NO ASHES FOR ME

VIRGINIA KATHLEEN BOYD

Westfeld Press
HUDSON, OHIO

Copyright © 2018 by Virginia Kathleen Boyd.

All rights reserved. No part of this publication may be reproduced, distributed or transmitted in any form or by any means, including photocopying, recording, or other electronic or mechanical methods, without the prior written permission of the publisher, except in the case of brief quotations embodied in critical reviews and certain other noncommercial uses permitted by copyright law. For permission requests, write to the publisher, addressed "Attention: Permissions Coordinator," at the address below.

Inquiries to SOS Seminars, Inc., P.O. Box 493
Aurora, Ohio 44202

V.K. Boyd/Westfeld Press
Hudson, Ohio

Book Layout ©2013 BookDesignTemplates.com

Ordering Information:
Quantity sales. Special discounts are available on quantity purchases by corporations, associations, and others. For details, contact the "Special Sales Department" at the address above.

No Ashes for Me/ Virginia Kathleen Boyd. -- 1st ed.
ISBN 978-0-9916173-7-1

*When you walk through the fire
You will not be burned; the flames
Will not set you ablaze.*

—Isaiah 43:2 (NIV)

TABLE OF CONTENTS:

Chapter 1 – Suicide 1

Chapter 2 – God and Me 7

Chapter 3 – Drunk and Violent 13

Chapter 4 – Killed in Action 21

Chapter 5 – Divorced 31

Chapter 6 – Not Vietnam Again 43

Chapter 7 – Abortion 65

Chapter 8 – Betrayed 77

Chapter 9 – Cancer 97

Chapter 10 – Why God Lets Bad Things Happen 105

ONE

SUICIDE

"Dad shot mom and killed himself!"

As I stood in a phone booth on that cool November evening with the waves of the Pacific lapping against the quiet shore behind me, I finally heard the words that I had waited my whole life to hear. I always knew they would come one day, and today was the day.

So far away was I from the pain and torment of the lifetime I had left behind, that I had foolishly thought I had escaped its grip, but here it was calling me back. Maybe now I could finally bury my tortured past.

The year was 1970, and I had just driven across the country to marry my young man who was stationed at Camp Pendleton. I had been in California less than six weeks, and we were married only one month (to the day) when the unthinkable happened.

It had been a busy six weeks since I arrived in Oceanside and began looking for a job. In those days there were tens of thousands of Marines stationed at Camp Pendleton, so it didn't take me long to realize that there were virtually no jobs for wives in this small military town.

Soon after our marriage, I began sending out resumes to companies further away, mostly in the Los Angeles area, which was almost seventy miles away. As the plan was hatched, I could try driving the seventy miles each way to work for the next four months until Ross finished his four-year enlistment, or if the drive was too far and too long, I could get an apartment in the LA area, and he could move back onto the base. Then when he finished in four months, we would have an apartment in Los Angeles, and I would already have a job. Then only he would need to find work.

As it turned out, my job search ended quickly with a great job offer at Union Oil Company near the Harbor Freeway, and this had been my first day at my new job.

It had been a long drive to work that day. I left Oceanside sometime soon after 5:00 a.m. and arrived at Union Oil after seven-thirty that morning. The first forty miles went quickly, but the rest of the miles were in crawling or sitting-still traffic. I could have read a newspaper in the stop-and-go traffic, and as it was, I ate more than half my packed lunch before I arrived at work.

The workday was long too. I was replacing a lady who was expecting her baby. In those days, most women were still quitting work when they started their "family", and this lady was no exception.

It was a tiring and strange day at work. I was already exhausted from the early-hour's drive that morning, and as we chatted, I began noticing that my predecessor was unusually curious about me and my past. She was surprised that I had driven alone across the country, and when she asked about my family and my past, she seemed to be probing to know more about my parents, my brother, my sister, my life. Without divulging my terrible childhood, I related some general information about my recent work history and a little about my family.

As I was sharing little bits of my past, I sensed an eerie quality in my own telling of my story. I still remember how captivated she was as I told her a little about my family, and how I came to be married and living in Oceanside. As the day went along, we must have talked about my past life for at least an hour, much to my concern about hiding my past. I have often thought of how shocked she must have been the next day when she heard what had happened to my family that day while I was there at work with her. My father was literally trying to commit homicide, and did commit suicide, while she and I sat there and talked. I never returned to that great job at Union Oil, and I never saw her again after that day.

Somehow, I managed to stay awake and mostly alert until five o'clock that day, and then it was back to Oceanside. It was already dark when I left work and got to the parking garage. All I could see on the on-ramp and the freeway was red brake lights. It took me half an hour just to get down the ramp, and as I drove those many miles back to Oceanside, I knew that the commute was never going to work. In retrospect, I know that God already had it all worked out anyway.

When I finally arrived back in Oceanside, I pulled into our parking spot behind the apartment building, and immediately noticed my wonderful new husband pacing back and forth behind our apartment. I could only see his head and shoulders above the tall privacy fence, but I could tell right away that he was disturbed or concerned about something. It was already after seven-thirty, so I just figured it was about the long day. I kissed him as I brushed by and went into the kitchen through the back door. After a few seconds of me rambling on about the commute, he handed me a yellow envelope that looked like a telegram.

As young newlyweds in a small military town, we were poor. We tried to get a phone installed, but we didn't have the deposit money or credit to get one, so we used a pay phone booth on the corner across the street from our apartment. On the rare occasions when we needed to make a phone call, we scraped up the change to use the phone, and would both crowd in there together to enjoy the luxury of a phone call. I remember fondly that we referred to it as "our phone booth".

As I held the yellow envelope in my hand, a cold chill went all over me, and when I opened it, and read the words, I knew it was something bad. It was from my brother, and it told me to call home. Standing in our phone booth, I dialed the operator and reversed the charges to my brother's phone number. My young sister

No Ashes for Me

answered the phone. My brother is five years older than me, and my sister is five years my younger. She was only sixteen then, and I'm not sure she knew what to say when she answered, so she just blurted it out, "Dad shot mom and killed himself". It seemed that my mother was still alive, and at that moment, my sister thought everything was going to be okay.

In that moment, I stood there frozen to the floor of that phone booth. I was stunned at the words I heard, not really believing my ears, but in my heart of hearts, I had been expecting those words for years. We all knew it would end badly, but we didn't know when or how. That is the experience of children everywhere, growing up in homes like mine, surviving day to day, wondering when the end will come, wondering if we will get out alive or end up dead.

My mother had been shot at three times and hit twice. It was a miracle that she lived. One shot pierced and collapsed her lung, and one shot hit her in her upper arm and one shot missed. Even in his drunken state, when my dad realized what he had done and thinking that he had killed my mother, he must have known it would be over for him, so he pointed the gun to his head and pulled the trigger. He was still alive when he arrived at the small suburban local hospital, but he died on the way to a larger trauma-center hospital.

Standing there in that phone booth far away, there was little I could do or say. After my brief stay in Oceanside, I was already headed back home.

TWO

GOD AND ME

I'm not exactly sure when God saved my soul, but I know He was always there with me as far back as I can remember. I think it might have begun when I was about eight years old. Back then, nobody at my house ever went to church. My mother must have gone to church earlier since I had been baptized, and I know she would have liked to go to church, but my dad was violently jealous of her every move, which kept her a virtual prisoner in our home.

I don't know how I got to go to Vacation Bible School, but someone must have invited me the summer I was eight years old, and I went, and that is how I learned about Church. It was the best week of my young life. We sang songs, and made crafts, and had snacks, and for a few hours each day during that brief week, I was away from the ever-present fear of being at home.

I still love VBS. Every summer I see signs posted in front of churches everywhere announcing the upcoming one or two-week Vacation Bible School schedule. Church members, and anyone they want to invite, can attend VBS and have a wonderful camp-like week free of charge. Every time I see a VBS sign somewhere, I thank God for the people who volunteer their time, effort, and money to make life wonderful for people like me.

One of the best things about my going to VBS was that I learned where the church was, and I got to know people who went there. Soon after VBS, I decided I wanted to go to Sunday school all the time. I began to get up on Sunday mornings, and clean myself up, and get dressed, and then walk to the church for my Sunday school class. The church was not really close to home for little eight-year-old legs. It was about a half-a-mile walk, along three or four neighborhood streets, but it didn't matter to me. Even though my legs were short, and the distance seemed long, I walked back and forth most Sundays all by myself.

During that year, I began to realize that there was big Church upstairs after Sunday school was over. Sunday school was in the basement, and I had never gone upstairs to the big Church. I was about ten years old when I decided to stay one Sunday after Sunday school for big Church. I really didn't understand what was going on that day up there. There were people standing up and then sitting down, and lots of singing, and a man standing up and speaking. I sat in a pew and stayed quiet and just watched.

At one point, people got up and began to walk toward the front of the Church. It looked like they were getting a piece of something to eat and a little glass of something else. When it came time for the people in my row to get up, I went too. I don't know why the Pastor there gave me communion, but he did. Nobody said anything to me, and I went home and went on with my afternoon.

Later that day, my mother sent me to the little grocery store up the street to buy something she needed for dinner. A couple of the teenage boys from the neighborhood were there, and they started laughing at me and teasing and ridiculing me about taking communion. I didn't really know what communion was. I just did what everyone else did. But I soon learned that I didn't fit in. Even at that young age, I understood quickly that I was a laughingstock, and I never went back there to church again.

Never mind though, because my very best Sunday school teacher ever, had already left the year before. Her name was Mrs. Young, and Mrs. Young was very old. She dressed all in black (like a nun) and at first, I was afraid of her, but soon I came to love her. Mrs. Young taught a small group of little girls. Even at my young age, I could tell she loved God and I knew that she loved us. When she prayed in our Sunday school class, I would close my eyes tight and listen to her pray. I never really heard anyone pray out loud, and I knew that God listened to Mrs. Young when she prayed for our little class and when she prayed for me.

I remember at Christmas time that Mrs. Young had a small Christmas party for us at her little apartment. She was poor and her party was small and sparse, but I remember how happy I was being in such a warm, and loving, and friendly place. In the spring, towards the end of the school year, Mrs. Young gave me the BEST gift I would ever get in my life. She gave me, and each of her other little girls, a Bible as a Sunday school gift. I still have the Bible. It is dated May 10, 1958. At the time, I was still only nine years old.

 I didn't know that Mrs. Young was leaving, and when September came, and Sunday school classes started up again, Mrs. Young was gone, and my little girls' class was reassigned to someone else. Apparently, there wasn't a good adult teacher available, because two teenage girls were brought in to "team" teach us or maybe just to monitor us. I didn't know where things were headed, but the two girls teaching us just sat in class and polished their fingernails, and talked about boys, and records, and dancing, and they never really taught us anything like Mrs. Young had done.

 Even at my very young age, I had already learned that Church was about God, and somewhere along the way with Mrs. Young gone, God had gotten lost in my little life. That might have been when I decided to try big Church. I don't really remember. But big Church didn't work out either, so for a while, I stopped going anywhere on Sunday mornings.

 But God wasn't finished with me yet. I was eleven years old when I went to a new school for junior high classes. The school was for 7th and 8th grades, and it was far enough from where I lived, that nobody seemed to know about the drunken fights, and frequent police visits to our house. During my first year at the new school, I overheard some girls talking about their church, and I realized that it was close enough to my house for me to walk there on Sunday mornings. Though I was not actually invited to attend, I decided to go to their church to try to find what I had lost when I lost Mrs. Young.

The Sunday school teacher at my new Church was a young wife and mother named Anita, and she talked about God all the time, and she mostly called Him Jesus. She was almost like a young Mrs. Young. She had had a baby born with a club foot, and through surgery, her child was healed. She considered it a miracle.

I never knew anyone before who talked about getting miracles like they expected them, or even anyone who believed in miracles, but after attending Anita's class for a few weeks, I believed in miracles too. Somehow, I began to think that miracles happened when people expected them to happen. The possibility began to occur to me that expectation and believing God were somehow connected, and it was about that time that I realized that "faith" was the word for believing in God.

In Anita's class, I decided to believe that God was really somewhere out there, and that He knew that I was someplace too, and that maybe I mattered to Him. That was the beginning of MY faith in God.

It is said that hindsight is always 20/20, and I think that is true. Looking back at those earliest years in my walk with God, I can see how He had His hand on my little life and was always leading me from one believer to another as they each taught me something about who the "Great I AM" is.

Along with the words in that first Bible, that little tiny seed of faith planted by Mrs. Young grew and grew in me until I learned that while God rescues us from others, he mostly rescues us from ourselves, and He makes a place of rest and peace for us all the days of our lives. Through it all, my faith in God has sustained me through the good times, the bad times and the worst times, even to this day.

There will not be enough "days" in eternity for me to be finished being grateful for the life of Mrs. Young.

THREE

DRUNK AND VIOLENT

They say that you learn what you live. While I think that means that you learn at home how to live, for me the exact opposite is true. As a child, life at home was more like terrorism than living, and I promised myself that when I got free, I would live my life totally different than the life I lived as a child.

That has borne out to be true too. For example, I have never smoked even one cigarette or smoked anything else for that matter, and I could count on my ten fingers and toes the number of any alcoholic drinks that I have had in my whole life. My fingers alone would probably be enough.

Even at a very young age, I promised myself that I would never live with an alcoholic or be one. The beginnings of that promise to myself started when I woke up many mornings to the smell of full ash trays and empty beer bottles. Sometimes I would go around to help clean up to get rid of the stench. I have a strong gag reflex, and it was in full force on those mornings when I tried to help.

The smell was not the worst of it though. The worst was the madman that my dad became when he started drinking, which was almost every day. Actually, he was very scary all the time with his controlling, suspicious, hot-trigger temper, but the drunker he got the angrier he got, and he often soon became a raging lunatic.

It was an everyday occurrence when I came home from school, and he was at home, that I would tiptoe around until I could ask my mother if he was completely drunk or if he had mostly slept it off. He usually crashed on the living room sofa, so he was right in the middle of everything, and we would all walk on "eggshells" trying not to wake the sleeping monster. Most days, I could hardly concentrate on anything at school, worrying all day about what was happening at home, and what would happen when I got there.

When he wasn't crashed on the sofa, he would sit at the far end of the dining table with a drink next to one hand and a cigar in the other. He smoked Marsh Wheeling cigars, and there was always a box of them handy. Sitting at the table like that, he would contemplate about the family until something came to mind that he would start yelling about. Then yelling soon turned into screaming and then screaming turned into rage. Then he would throw something or get up and kick something to scare everyone.

He mostly didn't hit us because he was a city firefighter, and he knew that if he was arrested, he could lose his job. He was very clever, and always knew the boundary lines. Not hitting my mother was a boundary line, and losing his job was his only governor, but everything else was fair game.

There were patches in the walls where furniture or other large or heavy objects had been thrown against the walls, and all the while he was destroying the house, he would be screaming vile obscenities. As a child on a daily basis, I heard the MF word, the GD word, the Wh word, the C word, and most other obscenities that anyone dared to use in those days.

Even while riding with him and the family in the car, he might get the idea that my mother looked the wrong way at a man walking down the street someplace, and he would start waving his fist and screaming at the top of his lungs while he was driving along. Though we kept the windows rolled up in the car, I often caught people looking at our car at a traffic light, watching him raving at us. I never wanted to be in the car with him, but sometimes it couldn't be helped, and it is a miracle that he didn't kill all of us, and other people too, while driving around drunk and raving. While he never got arrested, my mother would sometimes call the police when he got especially violent and she got scared. Somehow though, it always worked out that when the police got there, that my dad would manage to look innocent and my mother looked crazy.

I remember one dinnertime when we were all sitting down to eat, and something triggered him into action. He started yelling about something that I don't remember, and very soon he stood up in his typical raging fashion, and then lifted up high his end of the table. There were placemats on the wood table holding dishes and flatware, so the table was slippery. In an instant, everything began to slide towards my mother who sat at the other end. All of the hot serving dishes and all of the plates and glasses, everything, slid toward my mother and crashed around her on the floor. There was food and broken dishes everywhere. I especially remember a two-layer cake my mother had baked that day sitting upside down on the wooden floor. I remember looking at it and wondering if it could be saved.

In the meantime, full pandemonium had broken out, and they were both screaming at each other. We children had stood up and began picking up the pieces, and soon my mother ran to the phone and called the operator to send the police. Then she jumped in to help pick everything else up and clean up the place like we were expecting company. She was running around in a frenzy, while my dad became cool and collected.

Since my dad knew that the police would soon be there, he went back to the bathroom and washed up, and put on a clean white dress shirt and dress slacks. So of course, when the police arrived, my mother looked like the raving maniac and he looked like a calm innocent bystander. After enough visits to our house, the police knew him and what went on, and took him out to the patio to have a little talk with him. Soon they were out there laughing and sharing stories about something, which seemed like a useless waste of time to me.

I suspect that the police were always trying to diffuse the situation, but didn't they know that we were in prison here, purgatory really, and being tormented every day. I wondered always what would happen next.

At night, things were always worse with my dad. He would stagger home and I could hear him crawling up the wooden basement steps. When I heard him coming, I would hide under my covers in bed. I had a bedwetting problem for years because I was afraid to go into the hallway to the bathroom where I might encounter him. He usually didn't hit me, but he would push me around, and sometimes grab me by my long hair, and always yell at me for something, anytime, anyplace.

He was more abusive and violent to my brother before he got married and left, but even so, I never wanted to leave my bed at night. He did not sexually abuse us, but that was the only abuse that we did not suffer.

I remember one night that my dad tapped on my door in the middle of the night. It was long after midnight, and he was saying that he needed my help. I unlocked my door and followed him to his bedroom which was all lit up. There laying on the bed was my mother looking very dead. He had come home drunk, and had tried to wake her, but she didn't move. He continued to try to rouse her, and I could tell that she was still alive, but she didn't wake up.

Finally, he picked her up and draped her across my arm and shoulder trying to get me to hold her up. My mother was only about five feet tall, and I was a good seven inches taller, and thirty pounds heavier, so he presumed that I could hold her up and try to walk her around to get her to wake up. As I began to walk in circles holding my mother up, I hoped she wasn't dying.

My mother's health was always fragile, and she had prescription sleeping pills that she often took at night to get away from his rage and advances. She had had rheumatic fever as a child and ended up with an enlarged heart. She should not have had children, but she had four pregnancies with four live births, but one baby boy died the night he was born. The story was that a nurse had contacted my mother three months after my next older brother had died to tell her that a baby had been dropped at the hospital at that time. Anyway, she had too many pregnancies, and had already lost a kidney, and had a hysterectomy, so her health was very borderline.

Because I that knew she took sleeping pills each night, in the mornings when I was ready to leave for school, I always went into her room to check to see if she was still alive. My mother was always groggy when I kissed her forehead goodbye.

I don't know why she was dead asleep on this night. Maybe that was how the pills worked every night at two o'clock in the morning. Whatever it was, on this night, my dad thought she had taken an overdose, and it was my job to keep her on her feet all night until she came out of it.

No Ashes for Me

Even though I was bigger than my mother, it was still hard to handle her weight as we shuffled back and forth. My dad went somewhere for a while, and when he came back, he had a glass of pineapple juice with a straw. I don't know where he got the juice since I don't ever remember having pineapple juice in the house. Anyway, now I had to also try to get her to drink the juice.

Looking back, it seems almost like a comedy of errors, but at the time, I was really scared that she might actually die. I suppose that he didn't want to take her to the hospital where everyone would find out about a possible overdose and how utterly dysfunctional our family had become. All I know was that on that night, I believed that it was my job to try to save my mother's life.

By four or five in the morning, she was still groggy, but mostly awake. I was in high school then, and I always got up around five-thirty to get ready for school. It was almost that time, so I went and took a shower, and dried my hair, and collected my things, and left for school.

Looking back, I know that I got through that day, and all of the other scary days, only through the grace of a merciful God. I know now that then, especially then, He had His hand on my life.

FOUR

KILLED IN ACTION

I had failed 5th grade in grade school, but in a parent-teacher meeting, my dad had threatened to burn down the school if I was held back, and someone at the school must have believed him, because I was passed to 6th grade on a trial basis.

Because of my home life, and a not-so-helpful teacher in 5th grade, I had struggled all the time, but when I had this gift of a second chance, I somehow saw into my future, and I realized that if I was going to survive, that it was all up to me and God. I had no one else. I worked very hard that next year and made B/C/D level grades. When I went on to 7th and 8th grade at another school, I was clearly in A/B/C grade territory, and in high school, I never earned less than a B grade. I was elected to the National Honor Society in my junior year, and I graduated with honors at age seventeen.

There was no college for me though. I always knew I had to find a good job if I was ever to get out of the house, so I took the business program at school, and at graduation I was offered an excellent job in a large corporate headquarters downtown. I could have left home then since I was making enough money, but leaving home meant that I would desert my mother and little sister. Also, I was afraid that my dad would hunt me down and somehow drag me back home, so I just worked and waited.

Except for going to both the 11th and 12th grade proms, I was never allowed to date in high school. Since I never dated, it was a difficult task for me to find someone to take me to those two proms, but I did find a friendly escort each year who agreed to take me to the dance. For some reason, attending those two dances was an expectation that my dad had which was an exception to his "no dances, no dating, no boys" rule. Even as far back as 7th and 8th grade I knew not to ever form a friendship with a boy. One time in 8th grade, I caught my dad following behind me in his car as I walked home from school with my girlfriends. One of them said, "Isn't that your dad following us?" I think even they realized that he was stalking me. He wanted to see if I was walking or talking with a boy.

After graduation, my life was mostly about working and steering clear of my dad as much as possible. I had a girlfriend who lived up the street, and sometimes we would get together and find something to do on the weekend. One summer day my friend knocked on my door in the middle of the day and told me she had a friend who she wanted me to meet. Through the screen door, I couldn't see anyone but her, but then I noticed someone standing off to the side. I opened the storm door, and there stood a young Marine dressed in a light tan uniform.

I stood there frozen for a quick second and looked right at his face, into his eyes really, and when our eyes met, it was magic. In that instant, I knew, and I knew that he knew too.

I quickly gained my composure, and the three of us went out to the patio and visited for a while. We all sat there as I caught up with my friend, and learned a little about her friend, and soon it was time for them to go. Before leaving, my friend's friend, Frank, told me that he was being stationed in Hawaii, and asked me if he could write to me. I told him yes, and that was the end of that.

Frank did write, and during the next year we exchanged letters often, and as time and letters went along, I found that I was becoming very attached to him. The other change that happened during that time was that I was finally beginning to date a little. My girlfriend and I went to some dances, and sometimes I would meet and go to a movie or out for fast food with someone I had met. I was already out of high school, but of course, coming home after a date always led to an interrogation about where I went, what I did, what I did not do, the whole standard scary tirade from my dad.

It was at one of the dances, that I met another young Marine, actually a soon-to-be Marine. His name was Ross and he had already enlisted and would soon be leaving for boot camp. He also asked if he could write, and he did. His letters over the years came in fits and starts though. I would get eight letters in eight weeks, and then I wouldn't hear from him again for eight months. But over the next four years we remained friends and are friends to this day.

The next year, Frank returned home from Hawaii, and we had a whirlwind romance that summer. I saw him almost every day for his one-month leave. I still was working, but Frank would be waiting for me in the lobby of my building when I came off the elevators at lunchtime and again after work. We spent a lot of time with his mom and dad and visited with his sister and her family. Things at home continued to be frantic since my dad grilled me almost every day. I tried to spend less and less time at home to avoid the collateral damage as much as possible.

Soon Frank's leave ended, and he returned to Hawaii. Within a few weeks, Frank returned home on another shorter leave. He was being sent to Vietnam, and this was his last time home before leaving the states. He had already asked me to marry him, and I had said "yes". This leave was not a happy leave. We were sad much of the time. I knew he would be gone for more than a year, and he wasn't going to be anywhere close to a phone, and even letters would be sporadic, but that wasn't why we were sad.

The biggest fear was would he survive? The year was 1967 and there were servicemen everywhere I went. Some were going away and some were returning, and some that I knew, would never return alive. The news then was all

No Ashes for Me

about Vietnam, and it wasn't good. Every day, the local newspapers published pictures of our fallen heroes, and my heart was hurting as the time got closer for Frank to go.

I can still see in my mind's eye the day Frank left. It was a hot July day. I was invited to accompany Frank, his mom and dad, his sister and brother-in-law and their four small children to the airport. We all crowded into his sister's station wagon, and off we went.

Back in those days, planes boarded from the ground level where passengers walked out to the plane and up the steps. Frank was a change-of-life baby, and his parents were in their 60's. They were crushed to see him go, and I was crushed for them as well as for myself.

At the airport, Frank tried to steal a few minutes alone with me as we stood off to the side, but soon it was time for him to board. He hugged and kissed everybody, especially his mom and dad, and then he kissed me one last time. After a long hug, he turned around, walked out to the plane and up the steps. At the top of the steps he paused as he stepped inside the plane. I can still see the shadow of the doorway across his back as he stood there in that tan uniform with the hot sun beating down. Then he disappeared into the plane, and I never saw him again.

For much of the next year, I spent time working, but also writing to Frank and visiting his parents.

I really loved Frank's parents. They were old enough to be my grandparents, and I kind of thought of them that way. I always felt comfortable with them, and their home was always filled with peace and love.

They lived right next to the Catholic Church so when I visited, I would go to church with Frank's mom. I often stayed over on Saturday night, and found her up bright and early on Sunday morning making coffee and getting ready for church. Even though I wasn't Catholic, I always felt comfortable in her church or any church. Even from a very young age, church was a wonderful place to go, always better than home.

By then I had a car, and Frank's dad did not drive. I could take them to visit their daughter and grandchildren, and basically, I could get to their house often for a visit. Frank's mom knew that he and I were serious, and she really wasn't ready to concede that he was ready to be married, but she put up with me, and was always interested in any news I got in his letters. Anyway, I think his parents were mostly happy with the company since we talked about Frank endlessly.

The months passed slowly but soon his year in Vietnam was winding down and he and I began writing more and more about getting married. He would be home in August, and we would get married in September or October. Spring had come, and we were all getting excited about the short time Frank had left in Vietnam. Mother's Day was coming, and Frank had wanted me to spend part of that weekend with his mom, so I planned to sleep over that weekend.

No Ashes for Me

I went out to his parents' house on Friday night, and we visited and had coffee until Frank's dad had to leave for work. His dad was still working and worked at an all-night store. He took a bus into town and transferred to another bus to get there. After he left for work that night, Frank's mom and I talked and then it was time to get some sleep. When I slept over, I always slept in Frank's room which was small, but when I was there, I always felt safe.

The next morning, Frank's dog came in to where I was sleeping and nuzzled me and licked my face all over. It was like he was trying to wake me up. I don't remember him ever doing that before, and I think that somehow Frank's dog knew that something big was about to happen. His instincts were right, and that thing he could sense, was about to change everyone's lives forever.

As I wandered out to the kitchen, I could smell the coffee brewing. I sat at the table as Frank's mom was buzzing around getting breakfast ready. His dad would soon be home when we would find out all the news from the store that night.

Crashing into the peace of those few early-morning moments, there came a loud echoing knock at the door down the hallway. A sudden fear came completely over me, and my heart seemed to stop. In the meantime, Frank's mom was shuffling down the hall to open the door for his dad who might have misplaced his keys.

I slowly got up and stood at the opposite end of the hall and heard Frank's mom gasp as she opened the door. Through the doorway, I could only see the feet and legs of the two uniformed men standing there, but I knew they were Marines. She asked them if he was hurt, and they said no, and that they were so sorry. She was calm, but crying, and she invited them into the kitchen for some coffee, but they were all business.

At the same time, Frank's dad was getting off the bus in front of the house. He could see the military vehicle parked there, and as he climbed the stairs to his apartment, he already knew the terrible answer to his question. The Marines were still there when he entered the hallway. Frank's parents stood there and held each other and cried. My heart broke to see their hearts breaking.

They asked the Marines a few questions about the body, and about dates, and what next. Then the Marines left. After a little while, I called my parents to tell them what happened and that I was coming home. Frank's parents had their own grief, and I knew I was not part of their lives anymore. Soon there was nothing more I could do. I went home.

For me the days following Frank's death were a blur. It took a long time for his casket to come home, and it would be closed for his funeral. Frank's mother had a cousin who owned the funeral home, and he assured her that it really was Frank in there. Still, it was hard not to see him though. I had dreams for years that he was calling me in the night from Seattle.

During that week, I stayed for all of the funeral home visitations. I didn't know many people, but I saw many tears, and then finally, it was time for the cemetery. At the cemetery, I stood there looking at the flag-draped casket, knowing that I was just another mourner of a fallen hero.

Nobody knew how much I loved Frank or how much he had loved me, and it really didn't matter anymore. I was startled when the guns were shot, and then it was all over. I got in the car with my parents and went home with my own dead heart and grief inside.

I took me a long time before I really knew in my heart that Frank was safe in God's hands, and that God had a different path for my life.

FIVE

DIVORCED

I grieved for a long time after Frank's death, but the time came one day when I had a talk with myself about my life and my future. I realized that no matter how often I visited the cemetery, that he was never coming back in this lifetime.

It was hard to know what to do with my time after work and on weekends. There were no more letters to write or receive, and no more sleepovers at Frank's house.

Finally, I accepted a dinner date from someone I met through a friend at work, and then I met still another person, and went out on another date. During those days, I didn't have any real interest in anyone and was probably not ready to date again, but I was trying to move forward with my young life.

Things at home were worse than ever, but I came to realize that I did have my job, and when I wasn't at work, I could get in my car and go for a ride someplace when a fight broke out at home. About that time, a friend at work invited me to an after-work dance, and I decided to go. In those days there were lots of military guys at many singles events, and that is mostly who I met. There were guys my age still in college, but since I wasn't in college too, I didn't often meet them.

At the after-work party, I met a guy who was in his last year in the Army and was stationed nearby. He asked me to dance, and I did, and he seemed nice enough. There was no magic between us, but I had already decided that I would never really love anyone again like I loved Frank, so almost anyone was good enough to date a time or two.

We'll call my new friend Tom, and he was friendly and attentive. He took me out to dinner a few times, and to a movie, and once to bowling, things like that, and over the next few weeks, he seemed to be very interested in getting very serious–he had even asked me to marry him. Despite his feelings for me, it wasn't long before I realized that our relationship was not for me, so I screwed up the courage to tell him not to call me anymore. He was upset about that, and really wouldn't take "no" for an answer. Finally, he persuaded me to see him just as friends and nothing serious.

The holidays were quickly approaching that year, and Tom had been telling his parents about me when he called home. He was from out of state, and he wanted me to meet his folks since he was going home for a weekend soon. I really couldn't go with him since my dad would detonate if I went on a trip with a guy, and anyway, I was trying to figure out how to wiggle out of even dating him anymore.

No Ashes for Me

One day he met me at work at lunchtime and told me that his parents were buying both of us airline tickets to fly to his home on the next Saturday and we would fly back the following day. I thought that was actually very sweet of his parents and decided "what the heck". After I got home from work that evening, I told my parents that I would be going on a short overnight trip that weekend, and as expected, all hell broke loose. My dad was yelling and screaming and my mother was yelling and crying.

I told them that I was old enough to go away on a short trip, and I was going whether it was okay or not. Finally, everyone settled down a little, and my mother said if she could speak to Tom's mother to make sure we would be chaperoned, that she would then go along with it, but my dad was still cursing and yelling.

The next evening Tom came to the house, and from there he called his mother. She talked to both of my parents and somehow, she convinced them that I would not engage in any illegal or immoral activity while under her roof, so the trip was set.

That Saturday, we went to the airport, caught the plane, and ended up in Tom's hometown. His dad met us at the airport, and he was welcoming, kind and helpful.

The house was lovely, and Tom's mother was lovely too. We visited all evening, and the next morning we had a nice breakfast, and later a hearty lunch. As the afternoon waned away, it was time to return to the airport, and go back home.

Our bags were packed up, and Tom's dad was loading the car to take us back to the airport. As we stood in the hallway saying goodbye to his mom, Tom vomited all over the floor. He had eaten beef stew for lunch, and it was everywhere including dripping into the floor grate. I have never really liked beef stew since then.

Tom's mom checked his forehead and was alarmed that he was running a fever. Right away she said that he could not travel, and we should stay another night. At those words, I turned sicker than Tom. I explained to her that I absolutely could not stay, but Tom could stay if his dad would please just take me to the airport. She begged me to call my mother so she could speak with her to convince her to let me stay another night. I was shaking as I dialed the phone to tell my parents what was happening there.

When my mother answered, and I told her what was going on, I could hear my dad revving up in the background. When she told him the situation, they could hear him yelling three feet from the phone at our end. I finally told my mother I that was coming home, and I hung up.

Tom would not let me go home alone. His mother was noticeably distressed that he was leaving in such a sick condition, but we piled into the car anyway, and soon got to the airport and onto the plane. We had driven my car to the airport at my end, so I dropped Tom off at the base infirmary on my way home, and he said he would call me the next day

No Ashes for Me

When I finally got home, it was after 11:00 p.m. My mother looked like she had been dragged down the street, and my dad was still ranting and raving, which he had been doing since my phone call back at five o'clock.

With all the screaming and yelling going on, and after twenty years of living at home with this maniac, a ticking time bomb finally went off inside of me. I broke into a huge argument with my dad, which initially surprised him, but he soon got the upper hand and he forbid me to date anymore. Here I was, going on twenty-one years old, earning a good living, and receiving such abuse that I just could not bear it any longer.

Finally, I told them both that I was going to find someplace else to live and was moving out. At first, they were both shocked into silence, but then, my mother became hysterical. Suddenly she was fighting with me too. She was following me around yelling at me that I could not leave home unless I left married. The three of us had been yelling back and forth for many minutes when I finally had had it.

It was then that I remembered that Tom had asked me to marry him. I calmed down, and thought about it for a minute or two, and then told my parents, that if the only way I could leave home was to leave home married, then that would be just fine. I told them that Tom had already asked me to marry him, and that when I spoke to him the next day, that I planned to accept.

Now this was a guy that I had only known for five or six weeks, and I had already decided to stop seeing him, but somehow in that moment, marrying him seemed like a perfectly logical next step for my life. I went to my room, locked my door, and went to bed.

When I got home from work the next evening, everyone was tiptoeing around me. After a while, Tom called to tell me he was feeling better. I was happy he was doing better and I was happy to hear from him. After we spoke for a few minutes, I asked him if he had been serious about us getting married. He said he was serious, and so after explaining a little bit to him about all the hubbub last night, I accepted his proposal. We decided to get married in about a month after the New Year, so for that next month, I was on autopilot. Everyone who heard about my little wedding was completely shocked, but I was like a woman on a mission with full steam ahead.

A few weeks later, Tom's parents traveled to my parent's home for our small wedding, and after the small post-wedding party, Tom and I were off to the Holiday Inn for our infamous wedding night. I did have some reservations about leaving Tom's parents alone in the house with my dad, but the next morning we came back to the house to say goodbye to them as they left for home, and everyone seemed friendly enough.

There is not much I can say about my first "personal" encounter in marriage, except that today, it might be considered marital rape. I was still completely innocent of such intimacy, and things became so forced and painful, that I quickly wanted to run and hide. Apparently, I was not the only one who thought the evening was a big event

No Ashes for Me

though, because a couple months later, Tom went out to a local bar for a beer with my friend's husband, and then entertained everyone at the bar with a play-by-play of my wedding night. My friend and her husband were shocked and embarrassed for me, and I'm not sure whether the actual event or the later entertainment spectacle were the most painful. Anyway, that is how marriage started out for me.

By spring, Tom had been assigned to something called funeral detail. The Vietnam War was still raging, and caskets of our heroes were still coming home every day. Tom and other soldiers at his base were being sent to small towns nearby to serve as honor guards at funerals, and he was often gone for two or three days at a time. This went on from about March through early summer, and even though we were only married for three or four months, I was getting used to him traveling for work.

For the July 4th holiday, we were invited to a cookout with other soldiers and their wives, and I was happy to meet other families from Tom's base. The wives did not seem very friendly to me, and talk went from kids, to families, to work. During all the chit-chat, the discussion finally came around to the funeral details that some of our husbands had been assigned to, and soon one of the other wives was pleased to inform me that on those funeral detail trips, that my husband had been buying prostitutes. It was clear to me that everyone there but me knew about it, and I was embarrassed and hurt as we immediately left the party for home.

At home Tom assured me that it wasn't him, but was one of the other guys, but I believed the wife and not Tom. One time before we were married, I had loaned Tom my car for a few days, and as I came home from work on the city bus, I saw my car parked in front of a "girly show" theater near downtown. I knew it was my car, and I knew that he was in there. That was part of the reason why I hadn't wanted to see him anymore back when we first dated.

I was sick and shaking as I went to sleep that night after the July 4th party, and I didn't know what to do about it. I knew I would never go around any of those families again though.

During the rest of July, I seemed to be operating in "zombie" mode. I went to work as usual, and then tried to be civil at home, but I was hurt and scared all at the same time. Toward the end of July, Tom had gone to the store for something while I was sorting laundry to get ready for the laundromat. As I rummaged through all of our pockets digging out candy and trash, I came upon a slip of paper in his uniform shirt pocket with three phone numbers and three girls' names next to them.

For a frozen moment, I sat there looking at the note with my fingers trembling. Thinking I would confront him about the note when he returned home, I suddenly had a burst of courage, and went to the phone and called the first number on the list. I asked for the name of the girl next to the number, and it was she speaking at the other end of the phone.

No Ashes for Me

As it turned out she was a friend of a girl whose brother was stationed with Tom at the base and she told me that my husband had been calling his friend's sister and her girlfriends, and even had made a, trip some thirty miles away, to meet up with them.

I thanked the girl for the information and as I sat there stunned for a few minutes, I decided to call the girl's number whose brother was stationed at the base with Tom. By the time I made the call to the second girl, her mother must have been warned about me by the first girl. The mother answered the phone, and when I asked for her daughter, she informed me that her daughter and her daughter's friends were only thirteen and fourteen years old, and if she ever heard from me or my husband again, that she would call and report him to the police. I quickly apologized for her inconvenience and hung up.

I was still sitting there staring at the note in my hand when Tom came home. Since his Army enlistment was ending in about a month, I told him he would need to make plans to go back home as soon as he could leave, so that his parents could finish raising him. I decided that it was over. I was finished.

There were other disturbing incidents during my brief marriage to Tom that were alarming to me. Once I went to open his top dresser drawer to put clothes away, and he ran over and slammed the drawer on my hand before I could get it fully open. When I demanded to know what was in the drawer, he stood guard in front of the dresser until I finally gave up and went away.

Another time, he came home from the base after work, and the green Army fatigue uniform that he was wearing was all wet. He told me that he was in the stall in the bathroom at the base, and the guys there dumped a bucket of water over him in the booth. I had already begun to think that he was reading girly magazines behind my back, and it somehow occurred to me that his reading selections and bathroom habits might have had something to do with that soaking.

A couple of times over the next few weeks, when I insisted that he leave, he packed up a few things and was gone for a few days, but each time he returned asking for another chance. When he was back, it was clear that he was not changing his habits, and it had become impossible for me to continue living with him. We finally sat down and talked about everything that had happened, and I convinced him that it was over for us and that he had to go. I told him that he could take the car, and he only needed to continue making the car payments and that I would keep the furniture and pay all the rest of our bills. Since he was out of the Army by then, he agreed to take his things and go back home to his parents.

That Sunday I helped him pack up all his personal belongings and load them in the car. I had traded in my car, for the only car we had, leaving me without transportation, so I asked him to drop me off at work on his way out of town the next morning.

No Ashes for Me

I hardly slept that night knowing that I was living with a virtual stranger, but that Monday morning finally arrived, and he drove me to work, got out of the car and came around and opened the door for me to get out. I got out and started to walk away as he grabbed my arm and kissed me goodbye. He got back in the car then and drove down the street as I stood there watching him drive out of sight. I thankfully have never seen him again since.

After a few weeks, I was able to scrape up enough money to hire an attorney, and at the divorce hearing, only I was present as part of the divorcing couple. Tom had not answered the complaint or responded to the divorce in any way, so the divorce was quickly granted. I didn't believe in divorce, but I also knew that I could never bring children into such a perverted marriage and home.

After the hearing was over, I remember going outside and standing on the busy street corner next to the county courthouse and crying my eyes out. I knew I was making a spectacle of myself, but I couldn't stop crying long enough to start walking. Finally, I calmed down, and then walked down the street and caught the bus home, but on that day, I felt like the biggest failure in the world.

That day, my spirit was too crushed to understand that even in my defeat, God still had a plan for my life.

SIX

NOT VIETNAM AGAIN

Sitting across from my good friend Ross, a morbid chill went through me as he told me that he was soon returning to Vietnam. For a quick second, my mind raced back to that day in the cemetery with the flag-draped casket and the sound of the guns firing. I shook myself back to the present, and looked at this scrub-faced man, little more than a grown boy really, and I wished that he wasn't going back to hell.

I had met Ross at a dance after I was out of high school—one of the few dances I was ever permitted to attend. When we met, Ross had just enlisted in the Marines and was soon going away to boot camp. Back then, most guys my age were either being drafted, enlisting, or going to college. After Ross left for duty, we wrote off-and-on over the years, and he visited on the rare occasions when he was home on leave. I was amazed that after all this time, he was sitting right here close enough for me to touch.

Many weeks earlier I had received a letter from Ross that had arrived at my parents' house. I didn't live there anymore, but they were still at the same address. I tried to avoid going home as much as possible since I was still so scared of my dad, but one day I stopped in, and there was the letter. I hadn't heard from Ross in what seemed like years, but it was just like him to wander back into my life at any moment's notice.

In the letter, Ross said that he had been to Vietnam, and was back home again, and that he had been thinking about me. I was thankful that he mercifully had made it home alive, but my life was too chaotic for any long-range friendships just then, so I wrote back and told him that I had been married since I saw him last, and I discouraged him from writing to me anymore. Soon I received another letter from Ross apologizing to me for intruding in my life and telling me that he totally understood my feelings.

My life had become more and more complicated as the weeks and months went along, and soon I was working two jobs to try to pay off the bills left over from my brief but expensive marriage. I worked in the office during the day and left immediately for my evening and weekend cashier's job at Zayres. I never had time to eat between jobs, with only time to grab a hot pretzel as I put on my smock to begin my evening shift. By ten-thirty at night, I was dead on my feet as I dragged myself back home to my apartment.

No Ashes for Me

I had moved to a small place up the hill from my parents' house, and life at my little apartment was becoming chaotic too. Occasionally my mother would show up with a couple of brown paper grocery bags containing her personal things, and she would try to stay with me for a day or so. My sister would come there too if she wasn't staying with one of her girlfriends. She was sixteen then, and had a steady boyfriend, and when things got bad for her at home, her boyfriend's parents would sometimes let her crash on their sofa too.

I was fine with both my mother and sister camping out with me from time to time, but a big problem was that my dad knew when my mom had walked up the hill to stay at my place. After he went out and got drunk, he would show up outside my apartment at two or three in the morning and sit there in the middle of the street honking the horn and yelling obscenities at my building. My sister's boyfriend was also jealous of her, and he would sometimes come by, and they would argue out there too. Even in my own home, there was no peace, and my new neighbors were not big fans of me and my family either.

One evening while I was working at Zayres, Ross's married brother and sister-in-law came through my checkout line. Most of Ross's family had moved to the next state over while Ross was in boot camp, but his one married brother still lived in my city. Ross had taken me to visit his brother and sister-in-law once, and they were wonderful people who treated me well. I don't know how they knew I had been married, but as I rung up their merchandise, his sister-in-law noticed that I wasn't wearing a wedding ring and asked about it. I told her that my marriage was over, and I was embarrassed that she knew about my marriage and now knew about my divorce. I tried to be friendly as she and I chatted for a quick minute, and then they left.

Seeing them made me think about Ross and I remembered Ross's last letter that was in my stored belongings somewhere. After digging around a little, I found his last letter, and thought that by now he might be stationed somewhere else. I decided to send him a card anyway, so he would know about my chance encounter with his brother and sister-in-law. I hoped Ross wouldn't be embarrassed that his brother learned that he had dated someone who was now divorced. I did send the card but never got a return letter from Ross after that. I just figured that I was right, and that his family thought poorly of me with the divorce and all. I thought I must have lost an old friend.

Life for me continued to be misery. With two jobs, and bills, and my mother coming and going, and my drunken father coming and going, I was in robot mode most of the time, always doing whatever came next. One night in the middle of the night my mother called me by phone to come to take my dad to the hospital. It was one or two in the morning, and at first, I was alarmed about what might have had happened at home. Then she told me that he thought he had cancer and wanted me to take him to the hospital. He had found a lump on his back and was in pain, so I got up and went and picked him up, and after a couple of hours at the hospital, I took him back home and dropped him off. He had an abscess which they drained before sending him home. Just another middle-of-the-night family fiasco.

One day during this difficult time in my life, I was at home at my apartment when the phone rang. I didn't get many phone calls since I was almost never there, but when I picked up the receiver, I was surprised to hear that it was Ross at the other end. He told me that he was on leave from the Marines, and he asked to see me that weekend. He was staying with his parents who lived about 100 miles from me, but he planned to take the bus down, and stay with his brother so we could go out. I was surprised to get his call and was happy that things were okay with his brother and sister-in-law. We made a date, and on Saturday he showed up at my door.

So here I was on that day, sitting face-to-face with my old friend Ross. I was so happy to see him—it was truly a blast from the past. We were still both so young and seeing him took me back to when I was even younger. We sat a while and talked and for just a brief moment, my miserable past seemed to melt away.

The happy feeling was short-lived though as I listened to him tell me that he was returning to Vietnam. My mind was racing—did I hear him right? Even as he was telling me that it was no big deal and that he would be fine, a million clouds of doom stormed around me, and I wanted to get up and run away. Finally, though seeing him sitting there smiling and chatting as though nothing was really wrong, I began to get a grip on myself. It was as though he was happy to have found his good friend again and nothing else was important right then. I decided not to ruin it for him, and that we would spend our short time just being together again and just being friends.

When I first was divorcing Tom, he had left with my car, so I went out and bought an old junky Mercury Comet at a small, nearby car lot. After the first five or six weeks, the muffler fell off on the street at a traffic light, and I soon found that it was using almost as much oil as gasoline. I realized that I had really been "taken" by the guy at the used car lot, and I didn't know what to do. I started calling numbers from newspaper car dealer advertisements, and soon I was able to make a deal over the phone to trade in the Comet for a used '66 Mustang, which at that time, was only four or five years old.

Surprisingly, my dad was very helpful in getting me out to the dealer with the Comet for the trade in and purchase. That evening, my dad drove the Comet, with me following in his Bonneville. Most of the way, I was losing track of him in a huge cloud of smoke, but I knew he was still there because I could hear the roar from the missing muffler. When we finally roared into the dealer in a cloud of smoke, everyone on the lot stopped and watched, but the dealer still took ownership of the Comet, and I finally drove out in the Mustang without fear for my life that something would fall off or blow up. Of course, it was still yet another bill for me to pay.

So that day when Ross arrived at my door without a car to drive, I handed him my car keys for the Mustang. I figured that he could do all the driving all weekend, and that he could get back and forth to his brother's house at night. We had such a terrific time together that weekend. We went to my friend's wedding, visited my brother, and basically just hung out together. Ross asked if he could come back the following weekend for a do-over, and I said fine. I would be working all during the week, and he could take the Greyhound back to his parents' home on Monday to spend the weekdays with them and return on the weekend to spend more time with me. His brother welcomed him too, for which I was most thankful, so the plan was set.

I really enjoyed seeing Ross those weekends, but there soon came a downside. After a couple of weekends, I was getting used to having Ross around and I began missing him before he even left to go back from leave. We went on picnics, and went to see car racing, and visited my friends and his brother. We would go downtown and eat at small cafes and take long walks. It was always easy to be friends with Ross since he was the perfect gentleman. He kissed me ever so gently, and with a touch of his hand to mine, I knew I was safe with him and we would always be friends. Just being with Ross was like my life had gone on vacation, and I was learning that I didn't want it to end.

The reality though was that Ross was returning to Vietnam, and I was trying not to love him too much. Soon he would go away, and my life would return to normal survival mode. Far worse than all that though, was that I might never see him again because he might never return either.

The last weekend before Ross left, we visited married friends of mine at their house for dinner. Another married couple that I knew was there also. During that evening there was a lot of talk about Vietnam, and the ghosts of my past began to haunt me. When we left the party and rode home, I sank into a dark despair knowing that the next day might be our last day together ever. That last morning when Ross came to take me to the racecar track, he had a little teddy bear for me, a bear which I still have, and the whole day was bittersweet. I was trying not to fall in love but it was getting harder to let him go. The day finally ended when Ross handed my car keys back to me, kissed me for the last time, and it was all over.

The next morning was a Monday and I went to work totally despondent. I was working in a small building near downtown at the time, and an older lady and I shared an office. It was a long rectangular room with our desks at either end on opposite long walls. Even though we sat cattycorner, she was close enough to see that I was in a total funk.

Her name was Kitty, and thinking back, I realize that she actually reminds me a lot of Kitty from *Gunsmoke*. She was an older woman with grown children and like me, she

No Ashes for Me

was divorced. She had natural reddish gray hair, and she had a really tough demeanor. There were a lot of delivery men who came and went at our office, and she often hung out with them in the loading room like she was just one of the guys.

Anyway, she knew that my life was mostly collateral damage, and she had a bit of a tender spot for me. The first week after Ross was gone, Kitty mostly left me alone in my despair. I received a card from Ross over the next weekend telling me how much he loved me, and that he was back at Camp Pendleton, and that he would let me know when he had an address where I could write to him, which probably would not be until he was deposited back in Vietnam.

When I went into work after hearing again from Ross, I just sat shell-shocked. I told Kitty about Ross's card, and she tried to console me, but soon I just mumbled that Ross was gone, and I was sure I would never see him again.

Kitty had been through a lot in her life too, and she had a strong streak of independence always looking on the bright side. She pondered what I had said for a few minutes and then she piped up asking me why I couldn't see Ross again. I looked over at her completely confused by what she just said until she blurted out the words "God made airplanes, didn't He?"

Suddenly I was overcome by something like a ray of hope, and those words shot into my mind like a laser beam. At that very moment, a tiny seed of possibility began to grow in my mind then in my heart, and soon I was on the phone with TWA. Looking back now, I can see the hand of God working through Kitty that day. My entire future, my children's, my grandchildren's, my whole family's future might have hung on that one question from Kitty.

In those days I was penniless and struggled even to buy food, so buying a plane ticket seemed even less likely, but I called TWA anyway to see how possible it was that I could make a weekend trip to California to see Ross just one more time. It turned out that TWA had two perfect flights for me. The first was a non-stop that left my airport at 6:00 p.m. on Friday arriving in Los Angeles at 8:30 p.m., and a red-eye that left Los Angeles at 11:30 p.m. on Sunday night returning me back at 7:30 a.m. Monday morning. It was like a round trip flight from my job on Friday and returning me to my job on Monday, with a weekend layover in California.

The reservationist knew that I didn't have money or even a credit card, but she booked the flight anyway, and then transferred me to someone who took a credit application for me. It all happened very fast and I was clearly operating "in the moment". The rest of the day, I wondered what the heck I was doing, and began again to try to get a grip on myself. As usual, I went to my second job that evening, and dragged myself back home and then back into the office on Tuesday morning.

No Ashes for Me

That morning, the phone rang at my desk, and the lady at the other end told me that my credit had been approved for my TWA account, and that I could pick up my tickets at the TWA desk on Friday evening when I got to the airport. For a few minutes, I sat there totally stunned, but when I saw Kitty and told her, she just laughed.

While I was surprised and happy about the news, I suddenly realized that I didn't have "clue one" how to reach Ross. The year was 1970, and back then there weren't any cell phones, or the internet, not even personal computers. In fact, the only place you could find a computer was in big companies where one computer was the size of a small house. No, it wasn't going to be easy to find Ross to tell him my good news.

I called off work for my evening second job that day and went home from the office to try to locate Ross by phone. It was about 6:30 p.m. when I was finally speaking with the Bell Telephone Operator. All I knew about how to find Ross was the return address on the front of the envelope from the card I had just received. I told the operator his name and read to her everything in the return-address corner of the envelope. I told her he was stationed at Camp Pendleton, and that he would be leaving soon for Vietnam.

Back in those days, there was a telephone feature called person-to-person. When you called someone that way, you were not charged long distance until the other person was connected to you on the phone. Once the operator had the information from me, she said she would call me back when she had my party on the line. She must have been angelic since nobody else would work so hard for so little. Over the next three hours she called me back about once every half-hour to let me know that she was still working to locate my party. I don't know much about how monopolies work, but I can tell you that on that day, I really got my money's worth out of my Bell Telephone service.

Along about nine-thirty that evening the phone rang again, and this time the operator told me that she had my party on the line. I was shocked. Back then, there were tens of thousands of Marines stationed at Camp Pendleton, and somehow that operator tracked Ross down, and he was on the phone at the other end at that very moment.

Naturally, he sounded really surprised to hear my voice, but a little concerned too, maybe thinking that something had happened to me or someone in my family. I was thrilled to tell him that I would be coming out to see him that weekend before he left again for Vietnam. I don't pretend to imagine the many things that must have raced through his mind when he heard those words, but what he said to me was deeply touching. He asked, "Do you mean that you would come all the way out here just to see me?" Sometime later, I remembered that he had once told me how nobody ever paid much attention to him.

Ross came from a family of eight boys and a girl. His family was filled with wonderful people, but his parents struggled just to keep everyone clothed and fed. Certainly, they didn't always have the time and energy to give each of the kids all of the personal attention that children often crave. Ross had a set of twin brothers two years younger than he which meant there were three boys two years apart running around at their home. He also had a brother who was fifteen years younger than he, and there were a bunch of older kids too. His dad didn't have a car, and either walked or took the bus to work and even to grocery shop.

The saddest thing about Ross's reaction to my upcoming trip was remembering something about Ross's uncle, who was his namesake, and who worked for the airlines. When Ross left for boot camp, his uncle had promised to see him off at the plane, but didn't show up that day, and nobody else was there either to say goodbye to Ross when he left home for the first time at age seventeen.

I could tell by the quiver in his voice that Ross was really a little emotional about my coming all the way to California just to see him, and he told me that he would call me the next evening after he asked his commanding officer for permission to go off the base that weekend. It didn't seem to me like it should be a big problem. After all, I was only going to be there over the weekend. The next evening Ross called and told me that everything was all set, and he would see me at the Los Angeles Airport at eight-thirty on Friday night.

I remember telling my mother that I was going to California, but I had not seen my dad lately, so I don't know if he even knew I was taking a trip. In any case, I never got any backlash from him about it as I planned my weekend escape. On Friday, I took my suitcase to work with me, and Kitty and I were giddy all day about my daring little adventure. I didn't work my second job that weekend, so I left work about half an hour early, and was at the TWA gate in plenty of time to board the plane. I had flown before when I had visited my grandfather in Miami, but this was an even longer plane ride. When I landed at Los Angeles, I got off the plane, and there stood Ross.

We were both so happy to see each other. Ross got my suitcase, and we went out to the parking lot. Ross had two brothers living in the LA area at that time, and one of them loaned Ross a car to use for the weekend. Instead of going to his brother's house, Ross took me to Denny's where we sat and drank coffee and talked and laughed the evening away. By the time we drove to Ross' brother's house, it was after 11:00 p.m., and his brother's family was all in bed.

Ross was sleeping in the room with his two nephews, and I was sleeping on the sofa in the living room. His brother was married and had two little boys and two little girls, so in the morning the house was a beehive with everyone buzzing around. We stayed that morning and had a long breakfast with Ross's family, but then we were on our way to do other exciting things that day. For lunch, we went to Taco Bell where I had my first taco ever, and then Ross took me to see the Pacific Ocean. By early evening it was time to meet up with Ross's friends Jimmy and

No Ashes for Me

Paula at Lions Raceway, which turned out to be a very big and very noisy racecar track.

Jimmy and Paula were a young married couple who lived high up above San Clemente beach. They had invited us to stay over at their apartment, and apparently that was the plan for us that night, although I can't remember if I knew that ahead of time. After the races, we followed them down to San Clemente and sat around talking and laughing until it was time for Jimmy and Paula to go to bed. Ross and I were left alone in the living room which is where we would be spending the night. Ross being the ever-present gentleman gave me the sofa and he slept on the floor, but before we crashed for the night, we sat on the floor and listened to Rod McKuen records about "The Earth, The Sky, and The Sea".

That was where we were sitting when Ross asked me to marry him. I was surprised that Ross wanted to marry me, or anyone for that matter. The whole time I had known Ross, it had never occurred to me that Ross would ever want to get married. My experience with Ross was that he would disappear for months and even years, and then just drop back in again with hardly any notice, so I never expected our relationship to be any more permanent than that.

Sitting there with his proposal hanging in mid-air I silently pondered what to do or what to say. I knew that Ross was a wonderful friend, and I knew that I had indeed fallen in love with him, but I also knew there was Vietnam again. I was already married and divorced, and I had already lived through a Vietnam death. Those and many thoughts were racing through my mind, but then a kind of peacefulness came over me, and his question began to move beyond my mind seeping first into my heart, and then into my soul. While my mind was saying no, my heart and soul were saying something else.

In the next brief second, time seemed to stop, and I sensed that I was in this amazing moment in time. We were there together–two people in one place in one moment. In all of time, even throughout eternity, we would never have this moment again. If only I could have captured the moment to save for later, then I would have answered later, but somehow, I realized it was now or never, yes or no.

Thinking back, I remember that in high school, I had taken AP English, and had studied many great books and poems. One of them was a poem named "The Road Not Taken" written by the famous poet Robert Frost. In the poem, Frost speaks of "two roads diverging in a yellow wood, and he was sorry that he could not travel both". It was about a traveler coming to a "Y" in the road, and in the poem the traveler wanted to choose one path, but he wanted to keep the first for another day. But then Frost wrote "Yet knowing how way leads on to way, I doubted if I should ever come back." In speaking about the paths, Frost ends the poem with "I took the one less traveled by, and that has made all the difference."

No Ashes for Me

I wasn't thinking about Robert Frost right then, but I must have somehow known that I was at that place in the road where my answer would lead forever in one or another direction. My heart was speaking to me louder than my mind. Maybe the angels were whispering to me. Finally, I summoned the courage of my decision, and quietly told Ross, almost whispered it to him, that Yes, I would marry him.

Even as I spoke those words, my mind was crowding out my heart again, and I began to doubt that we would ever really be married. My mind quickly began to plan for another season of waiting for letters from Vietnam while my heart began to miss him. I did warn Ross that for me to wait might be for him, a jinx. I had done that once before, and it turned out to be a tragedy for the young man for whom I was waiting. Even so, I vowed to be his. I told him that when he came home, if he still wanted to marry me, I would be there for him. At that we kissed, and then crashed for the night, and soon it was morning again.

At breakfast Ross told Jimmy and Paula our big news, and they seemed thrilled about it. At least Paula seemed thrilled which was easy for her given her bubbly personality. After breakfast, we said goodbye, and left to go back to Ross' brother's house. That afternoon, his other brother and his family joined in a backyard cookout, and I got to meet everyone. Ross had two brothers there who had married two sisters, and they each had two boys and then two girls in that order. I was amazed.

While I was busy visiting with the wives and the kids, I soon noticed a little disagreement breaking out in the gazebo between Ross and one of his brothers. It seemed that Ross had gone AWOL that weekend to see me, and his brother was angry about it, and was also not happy that Ross wanted to marry me.

I didn't know anything about what it meant to be AWOL, but apparently Ross could not take off for the weekend like I had thought he could do. When Ross found out from his CO that he couldn't leave the base to spend the weekend with me, he decided that he could not leave me abandoned at the Los Angeles airport on Friday night, so when Friday morning came, Ross went to the mess hall, had breakfast, and then walked off the base to catch a bus to Los Angeles.

Ross was willing to live with the consequences of coming to meet me, but his brother was less enthused with me and our marriage announcement and especially Ross's AWOL decision. The rest of the day was definitely low key, and I knew that his brother thought I was nothing but trouble. Still the day zoomed by and it was soon time for me to go back to the airport to catch my midnight plane. This time at the airport, I knew it really was goodbye. We kissed one last time, and then I went down the ramp to the plane, and once again Ross was gone.

I got to the office on time next morning, and told Kitty all about the weekend, but still I was despondent. That evening Ross called me to tell me what had happened

No Ashes for Me

when he reported to his commanding officer that morning. Apparently, it could have been much worse.

Ross did not get kicked out of the Marine Corps, he did not get sent to jail, and he did not get demoted. His commanding officer was merciful in that he fined Ross part of his pay for three months and ordered Ross to serve an extra three days at the end of his enlistment to make up for the missed three days. Inwardly I was very thankful to his CO for his kindness, but nobody but God knew how that trip to California would put into motion events that would change our lives forever.

By the last week of July, Ross was scheduled to soon ship out to Vietnam. I got my rolls of film developed from my trip to California and showed pictures to Kitty and to my mom. Though it had been a wonderful trip to see Ross, I missed him more than ever, and found myself crying often when I was alone. Mostly, I was beginning to get that scared sick feeling for Ross more and more every day.

On the last Friday of the month, I was home in the evening when the phone rang. It was Ross calling me from a phone booth where all the guys were waiting in line to call and say goodbye to their loved ones. The guys were boarding buses to go to El Toro airbase to catch their plane headed to Vietnam.

What happened next was what can only be described as "THE MIRACLE HAPPENS HERE." Ross had only spoken a few words to me on the phone before someone tapped on the glass window of the phone booth and motioned for him to come out. I could hear some discussion from him in the phone booth, and then he came back and told me that something was wrong and that he would call me later.

Later Ross did call back to tell me that there was a mix-up and that he couldn't leave with his unit because his pay records were missing. I don't know much about the military, but in those days, the serviceman had to take his records folder with him to the next duty station, and Ross had missing records.

What had amazingly happened was that when I went to California and Ross went AWOL for three days, Ross had received a payroll fine as part of his discipline. After that, someone at payroll pulled Ross's pay record to apply the fine but failed to return his pay record to his records folder. Then when it was time to board the bus to leave for El Toro, Ross couldn't go because he didn't have his complete records folder with him.

There was one other road bump ahead for him to make that return trip to Vietnam. Ross's enlistment would be finished the following March and when he missed the buses that night, it was still the previous July. By Monday when everything would get sorted out, it would be August. Even one day in a month counted as a calendar month, and by Monday he would go from nine calendar months down to eight.

During Vietnam, the typical deployment over there lasted thirteen months but people could be sent for less time than that. There was an exception to being deployed when there was less than nine calendar months left to serve. A Marine would not be ordered to go. Ross never knew anything about that nine calendar-month rule until he missed his bus.

On the following Monday when he was asked if he wanted to go back to Vietnam, Ross told his CO that he would rather stay and finish out his enlistment in California. Since that change was approved by his CO, Ross called me that evening and asked me if I would come out to California to marry him then. It was shocking how quickly plans had changed in a few days, but I knew it was a blessing that Ross wasn't returning to Vietnam. I told him I would marry him, and we talked about how soon I could get to California for us to get married.

I often wondered what would have happened to Ross back in Vietnam. Would he also have died? I don't know the answer, nobody does but God. But there were a series of non-connected events that kept Ross at Camp Pendleton and I consider them Divine Providence. By early October I was there with him, and we were married. Our anniversary is exactly one month before my dad shot my mother and committed suicide.

It is hard sometimes for me to believe that one simple comment from Kitty about airplanes would change the trajectory of my whole life, but I can see now, that in that one moment, that God had put in motion events that would take me far away from the torment and abuse of my childhood, and into the arms of someone I would love forever.

SEVEN

ABORTION

As I sat there in that dreary little office at Planned Parenthood, I wondered how this whole abortion thing worked, and what exactly happened in an abortion anyway.

The lady sitting at the small metal desk across from me was rummaging through some papers, and she was handing me some of them to fill out on my side of the desk. There wasn't much in the way of paperwork though, but I did fill out what she gave me. I thought maybe there would be more papers to sign when I returned later for the abortion.

When I called to make the appointment for this visit, I was told that I would need a note from my doctor confirming that I was pregnant. I was told that I could go to any doctor and give him a urine sample and I would know in a couple of days. I did go to our nearest medical center, and I did have the note with me. She looked at the note, wrote something down, and returned the note to me, a note which I still have today.

It was late in June of 1973 then, and Roe v. Wade had made abortion legal about twenty weeks earlier, so here I was, an early-abortion patient, sitting in this sorry little office. It had only been such a short time since it was legal for them to perform abortions, but they were already up and running.

As I sat there, I was waiting for someone to come out to counsel me. I had been seeing advertisements about Planned Parenthood, and they claimed to help women with family planning counselling, so I was waiting my turn to be counselled. I was expecting to be interviewed and helped by a doctor, but it turned out that the lady sitting across from me was the only person I spoke with that day. I thought she was the receptionist. After all, wasn't this the reception room?

The lady in the reception room explained some of the papers that I had signed, and she looked at the calendar in front of her trying to pick out the best day for my abortion. We settled on a date in July, about a week or ten days later I think, and then she seemed to be finishing up. There was going to be a fee, but there was no discussion about any blood testing or other pre-abortion medical testing, or what they were going to do to me—no pictures, no charts, no nothing else.

Before leaving, I asked the lady about my counselling to which she looked bewildered. I began to explain my situation to her about how I had a 20-month-old baby at home and how we were really kind of poor, and as I was going on, she interrupted me mid-sentence. What she

No Ashes for Me

said to me next simply froze me in my tracks, and it made me realize how brutal this was going to be.

First, she said that I didn't need to explain anything to her. I didn't need to tell her my reason for wanting an abortion. I didn't need to have a good reason, or any reason. If I wanted an abortion, it was my right to have one. She also told me that I should plan to be there more than a couple of hours, and I would need someone to take me home. And "Oh, by the way," she said, "make sure to wear a dress". At that I was excused.

Leaving that sorry little office, I gathered up my things, and wandered out into the hallway in a daze. If I was really planning to have an abortion, I might have been more shell-shocked. But at least I was only at this clinic today to scare my husband into being happier that I was pregnant again. If it hadn't been for an unplanned pregnancy (both of my pregnancies were unplanned), I would never have known what really happens at Planned Parenthood.

As I drove home, there were two things that kept bothering me about my dreadful Planned Parenthood experience. The first was the lack of any form of real counselling. Didn't they know that anyone scheduling an abortion was feeling terrible and needed help trying to cope with the whole thing? Where was the counselling they promoted in their advertising?

And what was the thing about the dress? Were they going to perform an abortion with me still wearing my street clothes? Why did I need to wear a dress? Since I didn't have the abortion, I never knew the answer about the dress but the question continues to confuse me even now. More than that, I have been troubled forever by that clearly "in-and-out operation" with no consideration for the poor woman's physical or mental wellbeing.

Sometimes I wish I had never gone to Planned Parenthood and seen what I saw and knew what I know. I have learned however that my life has often been about God letting me go places where I shouldn't go, and about letting me do things I shouldn't do. Looking back now, it is clear to me that on that day, there was something that God allowed me to see and to know, and I have been pro-life and anti-death ever since.

After Ross and I were married, and after my dad's funeral, we settled down in California to a poor but contented life. Ross only had five months left in the Marine Corps, and we had decided that after his enlistment ended, that we would travel back east to spend time with our families, and to make sure my mom was recovering okay from being shot.

We weren't planning on having children, so I started taking the pills that I got at the base. I had been on the pill when I was married before, and I was fine then, but these pills were making me sick. Ross was concerned about how sick I was getting, and he told me to just quit taking them. He said that since he had been exposed to radiation in Yuma early in his enlistment, that he and some other guys were told there might be a problem with pregnancies. So, he thought it might be difficult for me to get pregnant anyway. At that I did stop taking the pills,

No Ashes for Me

and the months went by and I was fine, and never thought again about getting pregnant.

With the funeral over I was back in California and was working at a part-time job at a discount department store over the holidays, and then we were soon packing up to move back east. In March after Ross finished at Camp Pendleton, we loaded up the car and went to Los Angeles to visit Ross's brothers and then on to Seattle to visit another one of Ross's brothers before heading east.

By the time we reached Seattle, it was late March and raining all the time. We spent a lot of time indoors visiting while I was getting to know Ross's brother and sister-in-law and their two little boys. One day it wasn't so dreary out, so we all decided to go on a ferry boat trip. While we were out in Puget Sound on the ferry, I started getting seasick. I was standing at the railing trying to hang on and to not get sick, when my sister-in-law came over and stood next to me, and looked at me and said, "you're pregnant".

It is strange how, when we hear some words, they just have the ring of truth in them. At first her words didn't register through my nausea, but then I realized that in all of the commotion of packing up and traveling around, that I totally missed having a period in March. It was almost April and the last one was in mid-February.

Oh no, my thoughts raced at warp speed. Ross didn't have a job. I didn't have a job. We didn't have any medical insurance. Our apartment had been furnished, so we didn't have any furniture. The only thing we owned was this '66 Mustang that had started to burn oil, along with a few personal belongings, and about $300.

All of that crossed my mind in about thirty seconds before I started to cry. Ross came over to see what all the hubbub was about, and all at the same time, everybody found out what my sister-in-law at first discerned. My brother and sister-in-law were very encouraging and happy for us, and Ross tried to comfort me, but I knew it was really going to be bad for us for a long while. After a few more days, it was time to head east and try to carve out a life for ourselves. We kissed everyone goodbye, and off we went on the long trek back.

Originally, we had only planned to stay back east long enough to check on everyone, and visit my mom, brother and sister, and for me to get to know Ross's family better. We thought that after we had a chance to get our bearings family-wise, that we might come back west and settle someplace around Los Angeles near Ross's two brothers there. But now everything was different. I was already six or seven weeks pregnant and would be lucky to make the trip in one direction. From there, and all the way across the country, I had to stop everywhere to pee, and when I wasn't peeing, I was gagging. Poor Ross, what a trooper he was. We finally did make it back home with the car smoking by the time we got back with family. By then, I knew that we were at the end of the line.

Through the goodness of God, we were able to find jobs, and get an apartment, but we were still mostly broke. We didn't have health insurance since my pregnancy was

No Ashes for Me

a pre-existing condition, and Ross considered going back into the Marine Corps so we could afford the baby's birth. That idea didn't go very far though, and we ended up owing more than $2,000 to the hospital. In today's dollars that is more like $20,000, and it took us years to pay it off. Our baby was born in November, right around Thanksgiving, and I was thankful when he was finally here.

When the baby was only six weeks old, I went back to work again as a temp, with a wonderful older aunt watching the baby. We struggled all the time, and after a while I thought Ross was beginning to wear thin. He was working so hard to provide for us, and being a young husband and father, and with all of the responsibility of new family life, I was just hoping that our marriage would work out.

After the baby was a little more than a year old, and things had improved a little, I noticed a lump in my breast. I was afraid it was serious, so I called the doctor to find out what to do. I was on the pill after the baby was born, and the nurse called me back and told me the doctor said to stop taking my pills until after I could get in to see him. She made an appointment, and I would get a new prescription after he examined the lump. I did go to see the doctor, and I learned that I had a cyst which was the beginning of a lifetime of cystic breast disease, but there was nothing to do about it. The doctor wrote me a new prescription for the pill to start after my next period, but I didn't get another period and I never needed that prescription.

Once I realized I was pregnant again, I was worried that Ross would be mad or disappointed, or worried, or something. He already had enough to worry about, and I was afraid that this would change everything. We had just bought a little ranch house on his VA benefits, and we were trying to get on our feet. By now, I had a regular babysitting job at the home of a nurse, where I could bring our baby with me, but that was sure not going to last with another baby.

I didn't tell Ross about my missed period at first, but I finally knew I had to let him know. One evening after work, I told him that I had missed a period and that I was probably pregnant again. His reaction was a little muted, but he seemed kind and accepting. I was more used to the idea by then and was disappointed that Ross didn't seem happier right away. I was moping around about his quiet response, but he did assure me that he was happy about the news, and he kissed me and that was that.

As the days went along, I began to brood more and more about how Ross was going to like being a new father again. Maybe it was just hormones, or maybe I was afraid he wouldn't love me anymore, but I needed to know that he really wanted this baby. I continued to mope around for a while, and I didn't even tell anyone we were expecting yet. I wanted to give Ross time to adjust to the news so that we could be really happy about telling our families and friends.

That is just about where my life and emotions were when I saw the first Planned Parenthood advertisement that seemed to plant an idea into my confused mind. I decided to make an appointment at Planned Parenthood, so I could tell Ross that I was going to have an abortion–to threaten him really. I needed to know that he wanted this baby and me, and I thought this might make him realize how important we were to him.

I know now, and I'm sure that I must have known then, that this was a mean thing to do, which is part of the reason that it still haunts me so much. Even though I didn't have the abortion, the "counselling" appointment was also harmful, and I have often asked God for forgiveness for that time in my life (though I'm sure God forgave me the first time I asked).

After making the appointment at Planned Parenthood, I told Ross about it to see his reaction. He was clearly perturbed, but he didn't forbid me to go to find out about it. He probably thought it was just better to leave me alone with all my moodiness, and that things would just work out.

After my Planned Parenthood appointment, I went back home and told Ross that I had scheduled an abortion, hoping that he would try to stop me. He looked shocked, but just walked away from me. He didn't say anything else to me about it or about much of anything until the Sunday evening before the Tuesday abortion when I mentioned it to him again. I knew I was planning to call Planned Parenthood the next morning to cancel the abortion for Tuesday, but I didn't tell that to Ross. Apparently, he must have thought that I had forgotten about the whole

Planned Parenthood thing, because when I mentioned it again, he got clearly angry.

I wasn't sure what reaction I was expecting from him, but when he knew that the scheduled date was imminent, he stood there and composed himself for a quick minute, and then looked me face to face as we stood together there in our little dining area. Finally, he quietly but firmly said to me, "I cannot stop you from doing what you want to do, but if you do this thing, we will never have children again."

I don't know how long it took before I could say anything, but in my mind as I stood there looking into his eyes, Ross never stood taller or was more of a man than in that moment.

After I composed myself, I thanked Ross for finally stopping me, and I confessed that I didn't really want an abortion and wasn't ever going to have one. Maybe Ross never thought I was serious about an abortion, or maybe he was always onto me and my little scheme. Whatever it was, it was all over, and I was relieved and happy as we really embraced this pregnancy. That very evening, I called two close family members to tell them the good news, and the next day, I called Planned Parenthood and called off the whole thing.

Even though the abortion never happened, I have asked for forgiveness for even dabbling into the bowels of the whole Planned Parenthood experience, and I still must live forever with the ghost of those terrible memories.

No Ashes for Me

Our adorable daughter was born the following February–on Valentine's Day–and while God knows that she was always safe in me, just the memory of that Planned Parenthood experience, and the knowledge of what happens to children at abortion clinics every day, makes her every breath even more precious to me. I have often said that when she breathes in, I breathe out.

Over the years, with news all the time about abortion, I hear the rabid pro-choice crowd refer to children as embryos or fetuses but never babies. Don't they realize how evil they sound. There really is no pro-choice option, only pro-life or pro-death, and there really isn't a Planned "parenthood". It is really a planned NON-parenthood.

And last of all, those embryos and fetuses they are always referring to, are really sons and daughters, brothers and sisters, mothers and fathers, voters and even taxpayers. Just because they never got to see the light of day or breathed fresh air, doesn't diminish their personhood one bit. God holds those lives in highest esteem, and one day they will have their voice.

Finally, let me be clear that I do not believe that it is the frantic girls seeking help at those death clinics that we should blame for the lives lost. Those women of lost children can find forgiveness from God.

It is, however, the abortionists who should be looking over their shoulders watching for God who sees every abortion. The abortionists should be waiting daily for God's final verdict on their hideous behavior. Abortion is a business-making money by taking lives. There is really no disputing that fact. If left alone, practically all pregnancies result in fully-formed human beings much like my daughter, and most of the more than fifty million abortions were NOT the result of rape.

The blame instead belongs to the shrill huckstering by the pro-abortion crowd which makes their killing option seem acceptable to girls and women looking for quick relief from difficult circumstances. Does the abortion really help those girls and women, or does it really hurt them in the long run? And what about the unborn or never-born boy or girl. How much does it help them or hurt them? Only God really knows.

In my own personal experience, Planned Parenthood did nothing to help me in my planning as a parent. They did not counsel me, and they did not inform me. All they did was quickly "sign me up".

As I said before abortionists really are just hucksters selling their goods on the streets of our fears. The women are the victims, and the lost children are the prizes that evil steals away from their mother's hearts.

For me, I chose life, and I thank God for my wonderful daughter, and as I watch her life unfold day-by-day, I know that every day is a miracle.

EIGHT

BETRAYED

As I sat there on that park bench watching Ross pace back and forth in front of me, I couldn't figure out what was making him so agitated. He seemed to be wanting and trying to tell me something, but just couldn't quite find the words. Then he finally blurted them out. "I don't love you, and I have never loved you."

I heard the words, and I knew they had come out of his mouth, but I was still trying to figure out what was wrong with him. He fumbled around for a few more words to reinforce what he had just said, and then he began to wander into a long list of complaints he had about me over the last fourteen years of our marriage.

I sat there as he ranted on, and then finally I had had it. I stood up and told him that I was not going to sit there and let him insult me anymore. I walked away down the path to the parking lot and back to the car.

It was August in the 14th year of our marriage, and we had just moved back to this out-of-state location for Ross to return to a job that he had just left three months earlier.

Five years earlier, what had seemed like a wonderful adventure in moving away from all our family and friends, had turned into a lonely and displaced lifestyle for us, where all we did was work and go to school. We only travelled home to our friends and family twice a year, driving more than ten hours each way, and I anxiously waited for those trips almost from the time I had to again leave home to return here.

When we originally relocated here, we couldn't sell our house back home, so we rented it to a Lutheran minister who had just recently gone to Africa. Since the house was empty again after five years, we decided to move back home and find new jobs near friends and family there. So, at the end of June this year, we packed up and went back home to our old house.

Once we made the move, we busied ourselves in fixing up the house, while Ross submitted job resumes and went on interviews. I was happy, and the kids were adjusting well to getting settled back home, but Ross seemed angry and detached. I just chalked Ross's bad mood up to too much moving, too much work, and too much job-hunting. I figured that when we got the house fixed up and he found a new job, everything would settle down, and he would be content.

As July went along, and Ross was interviewing for jobs and at the same time working on the house, he seemed to be sinking lower and lower into a funk. His father had died about a year and a half earlier, and I know that he was still mourning his loss. But I thought that moving closer to where his mom and other family members lived, would be helpful for him. Each day that we were back home though, he seemed more and more restless and angry. He argued with me, and snapped at the kids, and I couldn't figure out what was wrong with him, still thinking it was too much stress.

One night as we were getting ready for bed, I said something that must have set Ross off, and he exploded into a loud tirade about how he was sorry that we ever moved back, and how he always hated living in this city, and that every bad thing that ever happened to him happened here. As I lay there in bed, he stood over me ranting on about everything that was wrong in his life, and then finally he left the bedroom and slammed the door. Suddenly I felt like a child again, back at home listening to the raving of an angry man from my past. I cried myself to sleep that night, not knowing what else to do.

Looking back now, I know that what I should have done was just leave it alone. The work on the house would have been finished, Ross would have started a new and wonderful job, and our lives would have adjusted into a new and better routine. But that is not what I did.

The next day, I probed a little to try to figure out more about what was bothering Ross. Since he had been so adamant about hating where we were living again, I surmised that he was sorry that we had returned home, and I thought that coming back here was one of the biggest mistakes we had made in years.

Over the next day or two, I tried to talk to and reason with Ross about what would make him happy again, and when I suggested that he call his old manager and ask if he could return to his old job, he didn't completely dismiss the idea. I told him that since he had just put the house into such good shape, that we could sell it, and we could find a rental and move back to where we were before.

After a couple of days, he finally placed a call to his old boss and told him that he regretted leaving, and could he return to his job. His position had not yet been filled, and his boss was happy to have him come back. He set a return date for the third week of August when we could get moved back there again. I called a friend of mine, who tracked down a house we could rent there, and then the movers came and took our things away a couple of weeks later. By late August we were living back where we had left from back at the end of June. Years later we used to laugh and say that we took our furniture on vacation that summer.

Now though, it was a week after we had returned, and Ross was back at his old job. The kids were struggling a little since they didn't want to leave home and family behind again. Our daughter cried for days when she found out we were moving back out-of-state again, and my mother was teary-eyed too. But we had put our old house up for sale, and I made the commitment to myself and to Ross that we were headed back to his old job, and that there would be no more brooding about being homesick.

No Ashes for Me

We were all going to make the best of being there, because I wanted Ross to be happy, and it was clear he was not happy being back home.

So, on that first Sunday afternoon, after Ross had returned to his old job, I suggested that he and I go out to dinner, and after we went out and had dinner, Ross suggested we take a walk in the park. That is where we were when he confessed his shattering news to me.

As we drove back to our newly-rented house, a hundred thoughts raced through my mind. I didn't believe for one second that Ross didn't love me or that he had never loved me. I mostly thought that all the moving and house fix-up and stopping work and starting work had taken its toll, and that he was just totally maxed out. I couldn't believe that he even realized how ugly all the things were that he had said to me.

Somehow, I got through that evening, and next day the kids were back in school and Ross was back to his normal work routine. However, after his confession that Sunday, he became more and more detached, and we barely spoke about anything but day-to-day small talk.

After a few days, Ross was coming home after work each night, with what seemed like an agenda of trying to clarify and justify some of the things he had said, and we began to take walks around the neighborhood just to get out of the house and away from the kids during those discussions.

At first, I had dismissed the things he had said back in the park, and I was waiting for Ross to get back to himself again, and to snap out of this funk. After two or three weeks of his detachment though, and the constant discussion about his feelings or his lack of feelings, it suddenly occurred to me one day, that he was serious, and this might really be the beginning of the end of our marriage and family.

When I finally realized that this was something serious, and that our marriage was really in trouble, I began to panic. The impact of the summer, with the moving, and now the sadness of our children, and the bills we had made with all the relocating, and now the abandonment that I suddenly felt, all crashed around me in one big pile. That morning when it hit me, I knelt by the bed and prayed and sobbed uncontrollably for what seemed like hours. I cried so hard and so long, that there were times that I didn't think I could gasp enough air for another breath.

I finally stopped crying and tried to make some sense of the impending danger. Ross had been telling me that he still wanted us to be friends, and that he didn't want to hurt me. I hung on that hope, but I also realized that he would have already left me if it wouldn't risk him losing his job. He was working for a non-profit organization with a morals clause that included strong family commitment so walking out on his wife and children would be immediate job termination for him there. He soon told me that he was looking for another job, and I knew that meant he was planning to move out when he found other work.

No Ashes for Me

During September and October, I was becoming more and more despondent when I was alone at home during the day. I had one really-great friend there, a lady I had met the first week we lived there five years ago. We didn't live across the street from her anymore, but after everyone was off to school and work in the mornings, I would drive to her house, and sit for hours and hours drinking coffee and talking and crying and crying and talking. My friend Fay was there when I needed a friend, and I will be forever grateful to her and her family, for her sacrifice of friendship during those dark days in my life. Many days her husband came home after work to no dinner, as Fay spent the heart of her day consoling and encouraging me.

As the end of October approached, Ross was still looking for another job, and our marriage was still on the rocks, when we got a surprise from back home. We had sold the house back there, and the deal was set to close that week, but our realtor called to say that the sale had collapsed, because our buyer's buyer didn't get final loan approval, and both sales were dead. At first, I was disappointed, but then I realized that my house was available again. Should we pack up and move back there one more time?

It seemed preposterous to move back into the same house a second time in less than six months, but we still owned the house, and Ross was looking for another job anyway, and the kids were falling apart with all the discord here, and maybe Ross could be happy there after all.

After dinner that evening, when the kids had gone upstairs to do their homework, I sat down and told Ross about the non-sale of the house, and that I wanted to go home again. He was disappointed about the sale falling apart because we needed the money to pay off the mover expenses, and other new bills. But then I could see his face light up with the realization of the idea of me leaving and taking the kids back home.

Ross said that moving back might be a really good idea after all. He said that since the house was empty, that I could take the kids and go home, and that he would continue working to pay for everything while he looked for a job back home, and when he found another job, that he would join us then. It was the happiest I had seen him in a long time, and I was all set to tell the kids. Within a few minutes though, he said he needed to run out to buy cigarettes, and that he would be back soon.

That was something else that had changed during this time of upheaval. He stopped smoking back when we got married, and he didn't really drink either, but now he was smoking, and he would bring home a six pack of beer now and then. Those were both habits that were also excluded behavior as part of his morals clause at work. As the door closed behind him on his swift departure to go buy cigarettes, it dawned on me that he really had a different mission in mind when he so-happily left, so I grabbed my keys and told the kids I would be back in a couple of minutes. I hopped in my car and followed him down the road until I found him making a call at a pay phone. In that moment, I knew I had been betrayed, and everything in my life changed.

As I drove back to the house to wait for him, my thoughts crystalized, and I realized that he was happy that I was going back home without him and he was there on a pay phone telling someone the good news. I also realized that if I took the kids and went back home again, that he probably would never come back too. He was seeing someone else, and I knew that if I packed up and left, that for the rest of their lives, our children would hear how our family broke up because I took them and left their dad. No, that was not how this thing was going end. If he wanted to go, he could go, but he would have to be the one leaving. I was staying put.

When Ross came back home, I asked him who his friend was on the phone. He knew immediately that he had been outed, but still he tried to convince me that she was just a good friend from work, and that there wasn't anything more to it. Of course, it was plain to see that he could hardly wait to tell her his big news that I was leaving him. He was upset when I told him I had changed my mind about going home again. As he continued to plead his innocence, I went to bed.

I don't know how serious his relationship ever got with his friend. Ross denies anything physical ever happened, which I am willing to believe, but it wouldn't matter to me anyway, since to me, that kind of relationship with anyone else is just push-ups. What I found to be truly destructive though, was that he was interested enough in somebody else, to throw away our whole family for nothing and nobody really. To me, she was just another woman who was willing to break up someone else's home and family.

It is hard to know who is at fault when a marriage breaks down. Everyone contributes good and bad things in a relationship, but over the next fifteen months, as our break-up played out, I knew that I had not done enough bad things in my whole life to deserve the way I was being treated. While he kept looking for another job, I went back to my old teaching job, and began to build a life for me, and for our children, always preparing for the day when he would get another job and leave.

Our marriage and family limped along for almost a year. Ross assured me that he had no outside interest in his work friend, and I kept hoping that things would improve. In the meantime, Ross was still at home, so I tried to make the most of doing things together as a family. Still, the breakup of our home and family hung over my head constantly like an enormous black cloud following me everywhere I went.

The next summer, I noticed that Ross was once again, getting more and more restless. Maybe he was being put under pressure from someone else to get him to leave me. I don't know. There were a couple of times that he packed up a few things and left, but he was always back home by night time.

Finally, though, he came home one day and said that he worked with a guy who had a house, and who would rent Ross a room, so he was now really moving out. I was surprised to hear that, since he still was in the same job, but I knew I had done everything humanly possible at my end to help make our marriage work. There was nothing I could do to stop him. It is true that it takes two to make a marriage, but I can say from experience, that it only takes one to break it.

That week, Ross packed up everything personal that he owned, except some tools in the garage, and he moved out. His closet was empty, and he had taken his new IBM PC. All of his toiletries were gone, and his dresser was bare. It was like he was never there. It was a very empty feeling having him gone after fifteen years. Finally, the realization began to set in that he was gone and that was that.

I was left with two wonderful pre-teen kids to raise, a job to do, and a life to build, so I started off by calling Sears and ordering some new throw rugs. It is hard to believe that God had a plan in using two small throw rugs to make it happen, but He did.

After Ross packed up his belongings and left, things were sad and looking a little bare around the house, so I decided to order a couple of fluffy throw rugs to liven the place up a little. Anyway, with Ross gone now, going to the mall that weekend to pick them up would give me someplace to take the kids for a little diversion. Ross had left by mid-week and by Friday, my rugs were in. On Friday evening, I piled the kids into the car, and off we went to the mall.

It is amazing to me how miracles happen. God always knows how and when to intervene in a crisis, and He has done it so many times in my life, that I can almost feel it when it is happening.

The "will-call" room to pick up catalog orders at the Sears was a little bare room about ten feet square with a small window at the end opposite the door. The kids and I were the only people in there on a Friday evening, and we were standing waiting for the clerk to bring out our throw rugs when I heard somebody behind me say "Hello". I turned around and was stunned to find myself face to face with Ross's manager.

I had only met this man one time before at a company picnic, and here we were standing there all alone in this small room with just him, me, and my children. In a thousand years, I wouldn't expect to bump into this man on that first lonely Friday night, but here we both were. It might have been just a chance meeting if I believed in chance. Somebody once said that "coincidences" are God's way of doing something anonymously. I call them miracles.

Ross's manager said "Hi" to the kids, chatted with me for a minute, and then asked me where Ross was. I must have looked embarrassed because I could feel myself blushing, as I stumbled to think of something to say. Looking back now, I suspect that he probably already had heard that Ross had left home, but still he acted like he believed me when I said Ross was at home working on

No Ashes for Me

something. I was ashamed that I was lying, but I didn't want Ross to lose his job.

After I picked up my package, I said goodbye, took my two kids and left. As I drove home, the kids were quiet in the car, probably thinking about what a bold-faced liar their mother was, and as I went along, I was getting madder and madder with each mile. By the time I got home, I was steaming mad. First, I apologized to my children for lying like I did, and then I decided to do something to correct my lie. I was not willing to own somebody else's bad behavior anymore, and I was certainly not willing to cover it up now.

After we all got back into the house, I looked up Ross's manager's phone number in the phone book and called his home. His wife answered and I spoke briefly to her. She was a nice woman who I had also met at the company picnic, and she promised to tell her husband to call me when he got back home. A few minutes later the phone rang and it was Ross's manager. I told him that I had lied to him at the Sears store, and that Ross wasn't living with me anymore, and that he had moved out earlier that week. The manager understood and told me to have Ross call him back when I could reach him.

It was late on Friday evening now, but I called the number that Ross had given me where he was living, and his work colleague told me that Ross was out, and he would give him the message when he returned. I called back even later after the late news, and his friend said he was still out. I told him it was a bit of an emergency, and to make sure that Ross got the message. I thought that if Ross was going to be fired, that I should at least warn him as soon as possible. It was very early the next morning, when Ross returned my call. I told him what happened, and to call his boss, and that was that.

The storm door was locked, and when I answered the bell early that Saturday afternoon, I was surprised to see Ross standing there. He came in and sat down and talked to me, and said that if it was okay, that he wanted to move back home. He said he was sorry for everything that happened and hoped I would forgive him. I wasn't sure what his boss had told him, but I suspected that two people might have gotten fired that day if Ross didn't come back home.

I told Ross he could come back if he was serious about being back. I was tired of waiting for the other "shoe to drop", and if he really wanted to work on our marriage and family, I would work on it too. I was clear however, that I was tired of being hurt, and I wasn't willing to let our children be hurt anymore either.

Trust is a hard thing to learn, but I think I finally figured it out. In some ways trust is like faith. Both are gifts really, but faith is a gift we get, and trust is a gift we give. God gives us faith through our surrender to Him, and we give others trust through our surrender to them. Simply put, trust is a gift we give to someone, and sometimes it is even a gift we give to ourselves.

Somewhere during the whole fiasco, I realized that I could never control Ross or his feelings toward me, but I learned instead that I could control my own personal life and how I felt about me. It became as simple as deciding to trust myself, and with Ross back home again, I decided to trust him too. It was a gift I gave to both of us.

The other thing I had learned was something about a crisis. It seems that the reason a crisis is always such a crisis, is that it is mostly unexpected, and we are usually so unprepared when it happens. As I was making promises to myself, I promised to also trust myself not to be so unprepared again. From that time on, I decided that I would hope for the best, but plan for the worst.

Again, I don't know what Ross's manager said to him that day, but Ross really turned a corner. Suddenly we were a team again, and he was beginning to behave like the wonderful, friendly and kind person he always was before. He asked me a hundred times to forgive him, but I had always forgiven him, even before he ever asked. He said that he didn't know why he detonated like he did, but that he was really, sorry, and I knew that he was. Over the next few years, and even now, it was mostly too painful for me to discuss the past, but from time to time something might get said about it. On one of those times, Ross told me that before we left to move back home that first June, as he was leaving the company and saying goodbye to everyone, his work friend had told him that if he wasn't married, that she would have liked to have known him better. It was really a small flirt, but it is strange that some small seed like that, planted so quickly in passing, would grow so big as to turn into a choking weed that could kill the whole garden of our marriage.

After Ross returned to our family, he was still at the same job and still interacting daily with his work friend which became uncomfortable for him. By then, the friendship seemed to have soured, and he was embarrassed to be there, but he still didn't have another job. By December, fifteen months after it all started, it was time for our bi-yearly trip back home to our families for the holidays. We had a wonderful time at home, and as always, I was sorry when we had to leave family and friends again, but we returned so we could all go back to work and school.

Monday was going to be the first day back to our regular jobs after the New Year. Ross's company managers always had various department gatherings on the Sunday after the holidays to kick off a new year of work. That Saturday I got a call from Ross's manager's wife letting me know that Ross's work friend had declined the invitation to their house, and that basically, "the coast was clear" for me to attend without being embarrassed by her.

As I stood there gripping the receiver, my mind went into melt-down mode. I thanked her for calling and hung up the phone just before the ticking time bomb went off in my head. I turned around and told Ross that the coast was clear for me to go to the party, but that I wasn't going to go, because I had taken all of the humiliation that I was willing to take in one lifetime. I told him that I was quitting my job on Monday, and that our kids and I were going home. Our house back home was rented out, and I didn't know where we would live, but on Monday I was giving my notice at work and I would be gone in two weeks.

Ross was surprised at my shocking statement, as he tried to calm me down, and figure out what had just happened. When he realized that I was completely serious, he suggested that he quit his job and go home instead, and when he found work, that he would send for me and the kids. For some reason, that made sense to me for about two seconds, but then I realized that I was the one who wanted to go home, and if he wanted to come home too, that was fine but either way, I was leaving.

The next three weeks were truly miracle weeks where we BOTH went in on Monday morning and quit our jobs. We planned to leave a week from Friday. The house we were living in then, was a small place we had purchased for me and the kids that April, so on top of all the other confusion, we had to do something with a house. At that point, I would have given it to the bank, but instead, I ran a for-sale-by-owner open house ad for the following weekend. If we didn't sell the house right away, we would list it the day before we left, and take everything we could carry, but leave the furniture behind until the house was sold.

It is hard to know if it was the first miracle, or how far down the line it was of all the miracles that God was doing in my life just then, but that weekend someone actually did buy the house. It was a cash deal, and we closed the deal six days later, on Friday, the last day we worked. The buyer gave us until the next Tuesday to remove our things. We were moving out two weeks and one day after we gave our quitting notices at work.

We rented a U-Haul truck and a car hauler and hired movers to load the truck. On Monday the movers came and loaded everything up, and on Tuesday morning we pulled out in caravan fashion with Ross and our son riding in the U-Haul towing our one car, and me and our daughter riding in our pick-up truck, towing a trailer.

I still remember driving over the last bridge as we left that city. Hitting traffic was like a snarling dog hanging onto our pants cuff, and I felt the tug of that place trying to yank me back.

But this time, as we pulled away, I was gone for good.

The miracles continued to happen as we got back home. We had decided that since Ross disliked our hometown so much, and since our house there was rented anyway, to pick a place on the map that located us about halfway between where my mom and where Ross' mom lived. There seemed to be a business corridor along that area where we thought we could find work. I had already called a realtor in that area, and I had asked her to show us houses for sale that were vacant. We wanted something that we could rent short-term, and then buy when we found jobs.

We made it home on Tuesday night, and temporarily parked our furniture truck in the driveway of our house that we had rented out. On Thursday, we drove over to see the houses the realtor had found, and we made an offer on one, an offer which was accepted on Saturday.

On Monday, we took our U-Haul to the house we had just rented, and that same afternoon, another set of movers came back and unloaded our things. It was exactly **three weeks** to the day since we gave our notices at work, and by then our house there had been sold, and we were settled in a new house near home close to family and friends.

It was the end of January when we moved in, and Ross found a great job in about six weeks. I also had a great job that started the end of May. Before Memorial Day, we did purchase the house we had moved to in January, and we lived there for the next ten years. The kids graduated from high school there, and finished college too, before we moved to another house.

Looking back, I can so clearly see the mighty power of God in my life. I think He had it all worked out for us when we moved back home the first time, but then He had to work it all out again after we decided to go back and live in hell for a while. God probably would have worked everything out sooner than those terrible fifteen months, but He was waiting for me to have enough faith and courage to step out and move on.

I realize also, that if we had done anything different, our children might have met and married different people, and we might not have our wonderful grandchildren.

Looking back with 20/20 hindsight, I know that God had his hand on my life through even those darkest of days. I had lessons to learn, and everyone had lessons to learn, but when it was time to move on, God gave me the faith, and a huge nudge, to move me along to our wonderful new life together.

NINE

....

CANCER

It was the evening of the 2000 presidential election when the hubbub broke out that started the Bush v. Gore hanging-chads controversy. I had just returned from the voting poll and was standing in my kitchen waiting for the phone call. I could still show you the exact floor tile I was standing on, when the phone finally rang, and the doctor was on the other end of the line. He told me the worst news I had ever heard in my life–before or since. My daughter had cancer.

It had been a little less than a year since she had gotten married, and she had just brought her baby home from the hospital a week or two earlier. The baby had spent more than a month in the neonatal intensive care unit, because he was almost two months early, and he had monitors and buzzers attached to him, and everyone had to take baby CPR in case he stopped breathing.

A week earlier, my daughter called me at work to tell me that she had a swollen neck on one side, and should she see a doctor. I looked up ENT doctors nearby and gave her the phone number of one to call. She buzzed me back and said she had an appointment for the next day.

The next day, I took off work and went with her for the appointment. The ENT doctor, poked and squeezed at the swollen lump on her neck, and said he thought it was just a cyst. She was really a twig at the time, so anyone could see that something was there. The doctor said she should follow up with him in six months, and we both left the office with an uneasy feeling about the visit.

The next day, my daughter called me at work, and said she wanted to get another opinion, and was calling the doctor to let him know. She called back later and said that the doctor had ordered a fine needle biopsy test at a location that was about fifty miles away. She could find something closer, but not sooner. At that news, I dropped everything at work and drove twenty-five miles to pick her up to take her the fifty miles, so she could have the test that afternoon.

The test was painful for her, but soon it was over, and we started on the long trip back to her home and to her young family. I assured her that everything was fine, and I really did think it would be okay. That was Friday, and I mostly forgot about the whole thing that weekend. But when I walked in from voting and got her phone call, I was alarmed at her news. She said that the doctor called her a short time earlier and asked her if her husband was home. My son-in-law had just gone to the drug store to get diapers, so the doctor said he would call back in a half hour or so.

No Ashes for Me

When I heard her words, a chill of dread came over me. I told her to call me as soon as her husband returned and they heard from the doctor. It was almost an hour before anyone called me back, and when the phone rang, it was the doctor which seemed ominous to me. He said he was sorry, but that the test came back positive for thyroid cancer. He said that it was a better cancer to get than other cancers, and he had already lined up a surgeon to remove her thyroid and the lumps. He assured me that everything would be all right.

My daughter was only twenty-six when she got married the year before, so she was very young to have cancer. After my initial panic, I knew I would need to get a grip on myself to be strong for her. I dialed her number and her husband answered. His voice was breaking as we talked, and I knew that he would be the key to both her and their baby's health and survival. After all they were all there living together all the time, and I knew that she would feel okay only if he was okay too. I felt alarmed at hearing the fear in his voice, and I almost demanded to him that he pull himself together and to "perk up".

Perking up, is an expression that I often use to get myself and others out of the doldrums, and it was all I could think of at that desperate moment. My daughter's husband is a terrific guy, and I could tell that he quickly realized what we were all up against. I am grateful even to this day, that he rose to the occasion on that day, and on every day since then. He is a wonderful encourager and protector of his family. After we spoke, he put my daughter on the line, and we talked for a few minutes, and then I let her go to take care of her new baby.

The plastic surgeon was on a trip to Peru, so we needed to wait for him to return before she would have the surgery. She met with him after his trip, but before he even returned, the operation was already scheduled for the Monday before Thanksgiving. My son-in-law's parents watched the baby the day of the surgery, and naturally that day couldn't have been worse, since there was a blizzard too. When she came out of surgery that evening, my daughter looked terrible. She had hoses hanging from her neck with drains attached, and she struggled to get on her feet to get to the bathroom. I stayed with her in her hospital room through that night just to watch her breathe in and out. After a second night in the hospital, she came home.

Our married son was living out of state at the time and had returned home on the same Wednesday evening when she returned home from the hospital. The next day was Thanksgiving, and we were thankful that the surgery was done, and we were all together, but we felt defeated and scared like dogs licking their wounds. It was difficult enough that our first grandchild was a preemie, but now his mother was so sick too. The two conditions were probably related, but that was never confirmed. Either way, we were all under siege that Thanksgiving.

After her neck incision began to heal, our daughter had to undergo iodine radiation therapy. Most people only have the radiation once or twice after surgery, but our

No Ashes for Me

daughter had at least five treatments over the next four or five years. Even though she had been sick, she wanted another baby, and had to "time" her pregnancies around the radiation treatments. She had two known miscarriages, but then finally with the help of a high-risk pregnancy doctor and the intervention of a good God, she was able to carry a second son to full term. He is six years younger, than his brother, almost to the day. Both boys are healthy with the preemie now being seventeen years old.

It was a long battle to get her completely well, but along the way she felt some new lumps on the same side of her neck. It was before she had her second baby when she found the new lumps, and while the doctors tried to do another needle test, they couldn't get the tissue they needed. Her surgeon decided to schedule a second surgery to go in and clean up any more tumors, and maybe take out more lymph nodes in her neck. The second procedure would be more radical, but anything he needed to do was worth it to save her life.

The day before her second surgery was a Sunday, and she was visiting at our house. She was sitting on the sofa and asked me if I would pray for her. I was never really good at "out-loud" praying, but I said sure, and we stood up facing one another. I put both hands on the sides of her neck, and I said a quick prayer, nothing really fancy that would make God sit up and take notice. Like I said, I wasn't very good at praying in public. But during the prayer, I was thinking how hot the side of her neck was where the cancer was, and when we sat back down, she asked me why my hand was so hot. I was wondering about that myself.

I believe in miracles, but I don't dare to demand or even to mostly expect them. I know that "expectation" is part of faith, but I also know, through many life trials that God works His plan in so many ways, that I need to just ask and trust.

The next day we all trooped back to the hospital. The doctor told us that the surgery would take about four hours, and he assured us that he would do a good job. My husband, our son-in-law, and I were there in the waiting area as the surgery began, and soon I leaned over and fell asleep. It wasn't very long later, that I heard the surgeon's booming voice. He was a fabulous surgeon, and did an amazing job on her first operation, but he had a loud and demanding voice which just then scared me awake.

As I jumped awake, I knew it had only been an hour or so since I fell asleep, and the first thought that came to me, was that something had happened to my daughter in surgery. As I tried to focus on what was going on, I could see that the surgeon was smiling and shaking hands with the men and was saying that there was no cancer. He said that cut nerves sometimes grow little balls at their ends, and that those little balls that formed on the cut nerves from the original cancer surgery, were the new lumps that everyone could feel. He had closed her up, and when she was awake enough to leave, we took her home that day.

It was really a miracle to me. Had God healed her yesterday when we prayed together, or was there never more cancer? I don't know the answer, but I do know that even if the surgeon had found more cancer that day, that God was still in Heaven, and somehow, He would care for my daughter and help me make sense of one more trouble to overcome through His amazing grace.

In the years since then, I myself have had a case of early-diagnosed breast cancer. When the doctor told me that my biopsy had come back positive, I told her to tell me what to do, and I would do whatever it was. I could cope with my own disease a thousand times easier than having my young daughter start out her marriage and new family fighting cancer herself.

Sometimes I think about dying, more so as I get older, and while the unknown can be daunting, I know it is merciful and gracious that we all get an escape hatch out of this life. If it were not for death, we would have Hitler, and Mussolini, and Jack-the-Ripper and all of the other diabolical monsters of every era, still with us, and would we want to live forever in a world with them.

Even all of us ordinary "good" people do not begin to be good enough for the perfect "world" that is waiting in Heaven. But the invitation has been extended by God for us to join Him there. It is open to everyone who asks to be made "good" by God Himself through the righteousness and sacrifice of Jesus Christ.

Anyone who chooses to believe in God's redemption and resurrection through His Son Jesus, He promises to clean up and make ready for the greatest graduation of all time. We can be sure that when we get there, there won't be any more suicides, or abortions, or divorces, or cancer, or any other scary monsters that make us tremble and cry. I myself look forward to that day, and am not expecting even a blip, as I go from here to there.

TEN

WHY DOES GOD LET BAD THINGS HAPPEN?

I have had a lifetime of hearing people ask how a good God can let such bad things happen and I can't understand why it is such a mystery to everyone.

We all know that lots of bad things happen to people all the time. If they really stop to think about it, most people have at least one bad thing happen every day. An unexpected bill comes in the mail, or a dinner date cancels, or a tire goes flat. One reason that people are so maxed out all the time is that we can hardly keep up with all the bad things that happen in our lives each day.

Sometimes though, worse things happen–really bad things–like a fatal car accident, or a heart attack, or a big fire. It is at those times that we often hear someone ask how a good God can let such a bad thing happen.

It might seem then that God is heartless or to some, that maybe He isn't even there, but the real answer to the question started back at the beginning of creation.

It is indeed a fact that God is good, so good in fact that He trusts us with our own free will. That is why Adam and Eve made such a mess of things. They had free will to make their own choices and they chose to disobey.

If someone scratches a plate used to print money at the U. S. Mint, every dollar printed from that plate would have the same scratch. Like that plate, Adam and Eve's sin is printed in the DNA of every person born after them which gets down to you and to me. We are born sinful because of Adam and Eve's choice to disobey.

In our lives today, people seem obsessed with their right to choose, but God was way ahead of those demands back when he first created us. In giving us our right to make choices, we unfortunately do whatever the "hell" we want to do most of the time. We make messes by our choices, and then we want to blame God for the bad results.

It should be clear that every bad outcome has its beginning in some bad choice someplace. It may not even be the choice of the person enduring the bad outcome. It may be someone else's bad choice that creates the mess.

Maybe someone at a factory upstream, dumps chemicals in the river. Soon the polluted water causes an epidemic of cancer deaths in a whole town downstream. Was it the fault of the people who died? Probably not, but it was indeed the fault and the result of the bad behavior of someone, likely someone upstream there at that factory. God calls it sin, but if it helps you to think of it as just a bad choice, fine with me. Just remember that it was still something bad that someone did.

Abortion is another example. You already know my own personal experience on that topic, but does anyone really doubt that an embryo grows into a fetus and a fetus grows into a baby, and that baby will likely grow into a fine man or woman? Going a step further, that man or woman may one day be the very person who finds the cure for cancer. Yet we all sit around, and pliantly agree that a woman should have her right to choose, without demanding that the embryo should also have his or her right to choose as well.

So while we live in a world with of us all making bad choices all of the time, we should stop blaming God, and when we finally figure out that we are the problem, we should also know that God loved us all the time we were making those messes, and He stands always ready to forgive our disobedience and clean us up.

I once heard it said that:

> "There is nothing I can do to make God love me ANY MORE,
> and there is nothing I can do to make God love me ANY LESS".

God's love is complete and eternal, because GOD IS LOVE.

Because of my dad's suicide, I have said many times to people, especially young people, to never do anything desperate in a desperate situation. There is always help-to-be-had. Call the police, or go to a fire department, or call a help line. Whatever you do, stop and don't act in desperation. You see, life happens day by day and something wonderful may be waiting for you just around the corner. You wouldn't want to miss out on it by hurting someone or hurting yourself.

I have learned through a lifetime of my own hurts and sorrows that God works in surprising and amazing ways. I hope that by you reading about my stormy but wonderful life, that you might be inspired in your own life to look inward, and then to look upward, where you will find God. When you find Him, you should be prepared to be surprised at how wise and good God is in that, through His Son Jesus Christ, He can forgive your past and redeem your future.

ABOUT THE AUTHOR

Virginia Kathleen Boyd has lived in various parts of the US, including the west coast, the south, and the northeast. She worked as analyst for large corporations for much of her career, also having taught college classes over thirteen years.

www.ingramcontent.com/pod-product-compliance
Lightning Source LLC
Chambersburg PA
CBHW020427010526
44118CB00010B/465